NEW VARIETIES

OF

GOLD AND SILVER COINS,

COUNTERFEIT COINS, AND BULLION;

WITH MINT VALUES.

SECOND EDITION,
REARRANGED, WITH NUMEROUS ADDITIONS.

BY

JACOB R. ECKFELDT AND WILLIAM E. DU BOIS,
ASSAYERS OF THE MINT OF THE UNITED STATES.

TO WHICH IS ADDED,
A BRIEF ACCOUNT OF THE COLLECTION OF COINS BELONGING TO THE MINT.
SECOND EDITION, ENLARGED.
BY WILLIAM E. DU BOIS.

NEW YORK:
GEORGE P. PUTNAM, 155 BROADWAY.
1851.

INTRODUCTION.

A SMALL volume was published by the Assayers of the Mint of the United States, in the early part of the last year (1850), entitled, "New Varieties of Coins and Bullion." It was designed as a convenient and authentic manual for individuals or institutions dealing in the precious metals, and especially those engaged in the California trade, then newly opened. It also served the purpose of a supplement to a larger work by the same authors on the same subject, issued in 1842. As a separate publication, the edition was exhausted in a few months. The lapse of time and change of circumstances have required that it should be taken apart, reconstructed, and in various respects essentially altered; of course with a view to improvement, and to making the book as fresh as possible.

There is appended a reprint of the "Pledges of History; or, A Brief Account of the Collection of Coins belonging to the Mint of the United States," which was issued by the Assistant Assayer in 1846, and of which scarcely a copy remains. Some interesting additions are made to this branch also; and the volume thus made up will, it is hoped, prove serviceable both to the man of business and to the lover of the curious.

ASSAY OFFICE, U. S. MINT, *September*, 1851.

CONTENTS.

NEW VARIETIES OF GOLD AND SILVER COINS AND BULLION.

By JACOB R. ECKFELDT and WILLIAM E. DUBOIS.

ASSAYERS OF THE UNITED STATES MINT.

Contents.

Part Second.

NEW VARIETIES OF GOLD AND SILVER COINS AND BULLION.

By Jacob R. Eckfeldt and William E. Dubois,

ASSAYERS OF THE UNITED STATES MINT.

I. — Recent Coins of the World.

A coin, once set in circulation, retains its place and use longer than any other part of the machinery of life, and is extremely slow in going out of fashion; so that the information respecting it, which the dealer, the collector, and the public at large require, does not soon become obsolete.

Pieces are current amongst us, a full century old; and all that space of time is included in the history of coinage, contained in our larger manual. But new coins, or modifications of old ones, are continually appearing; and in the latter case, it often happens that the holder finds he has become, if we may so speak, an unconscious sufferer. Old names are retained, but essential properties are altered; and a new progeny of doubloons, dollars, francs, or shillings, is found by an assayer's scrutiny to be something different, most likely inferior, to the older stock. Keeping a steady watch on these, as it is impliedly our duty, we have collected a number of items, which, as in our former publication, will be set forth in alphabetical order, and as briefly as possible. The weight is expressed in grains, and the fineness in thousandth parts.

Belgium. — Gold coin, 25 francs; a new denomination; 1848 is the earliest date noticed. It expresses on its reverse the intended standards, 7.915 grammes (equal to 122.12 troy grains), 900 fine. The average of twenty pieces tried, is 121.9, fineness 899; value $ 4.72. This is a slight depreciation: it ought to be $ 4.79, to compare with the former series of Belgian gold coin, or $ 4.81, to be equivalent with the French. We notice also, in silver, a piece of 2½ francs, 1849, weighing 192 grains; fineness (of a single specimen) 901; value 46½ cents.

Bolivia. — The dollars from 1841 to 1846, tried in parcels, vary in fineness from 896 to 901; a very large lot gave 897; showing some tendency downward. Weight, varying from 411 to 421, averages 416½; value on a general average, 100.6 cents.

BRITAIN. — The new *florin*, or two-shilling piece, being one tenth of a pound sterling, is understood to be an advance towards a decimal system. A considerable number have been coined, and the piece is fairly in circulation; but, like other silver coins of that country, it seldom makes its way out of the realm.

CALIFORNIA. See *United States.*

CENTRAL AMERICA. — It is not easy to keep pace with the fluctuations in the coinage of this country, any more than with its political history. Nine years ago, we averaged the doubloon at $ 14.96, and the dollar at $ 1.00.1. The country now seems to be divided (we judge by the coins) into two distinct republics, — Central America and Costa Rica.

Of the recent *gold* coinage of Central America, we have had opportunities of examining the quarter-doubloon, the eighth or escudo, and the sixteenth. The first, 1850, weighed 97 grains, fineness 863, value $ 3.60. The second, 1844 to 1849, 48 grains, 809 fine, value $ 1.67. The third, 1825 to 1849, 24 grains, 809 fine, value 83½ cents. — In *silver*, the dollar of 1847 is found to vary from 880 to 820 thousandths in fineness; those of 1840 to 1842 averaged 887. It would therefore not be safe to give more than 92 cents for a single piece, or 95 by the quantity; the laws of wholesale and retail, in the coin market, being directly opposite to those in other branches of trade.

The coins of Costa Rica, the seceding state, are in several respects quite remarkable; and in this particularly, that the gold pieces are among the handsomest that are current in the world, while the silver are beyond comparison the rudest; at least, the samples that we have seen. The specimens assayed here lately are the half-doubloon, weighing 208 grains, 851 fine, value $ 7.62; and the quarter-doubloon, 97 grains, 845 fine, value $ 3.53. The silver piece is the *real* (apparently shaped with hammer and chisel), 1846, 29 to 45 grains, 550 to 637 fine; average value $5\frac{8}{10}$ cents.

CHILI. — In the dollar of 1848 we find a variation of weight from 415 to 419; fineness 901½, which is lower than former dates; but the average value is 101 cents.

Until lately, we had no opportunity of testing the fractional coins. The quarter-dollar, 1843 – 1845, weighs only 92, but is 903 fine; the eighth, or *real*, is strictly proportional. Values respectively, 22.4 and 11.2 cents; making a profit to government, and a loss to holders, of about eleven per cent.

The newspapers of the day contain the following statement, concerning which we have no other information: —

" The Chilian Congress, now in session, has passed a new coinage law, article 1st of which states that three classes of gold are to be coined, of the standard of nine tenths fine, to be denominated, respectively, Condor, Doubloon (doblon), and Escudo.

" 1. The Condor to weigh three hundred and five $\frac{500}{1000}$ grains, and to correspond in value with ten silver dollars.

" 2. The Doubloon to weigh one hundred and fifty-two $\frac{750}{1000}$ grains, and to correspond in value with five silver dollars.

"3. The Escudo to weigh sixty-one $\frac{108}{1000}$ grains, and be of the value of two silver dollars.

"Art. 2d. There shall be five classes of silver money, also of the standard of nine tenths fine, viz.: —

"A Dollar, weighing five hundred $\frac{768}{1000}$ grains, and divided into hundredth parts or cents.

"A piece of fifty cents, containing two hundred and fifty $\frac{384}{1000}$ grains.

"One of twenty cents, with one hundred $\frac{155}{1000}$ grains.

"One of ten cents, with fifty $\frac{75}{1000}$ grains.

"One of five cents, with twenty-five $\frac{38}{1000}$ grains.

"Art. 3d. Establishes two classes of copper coinage, to be termed cents and half-cents, to be composed of pure copper without any alloy."

CHINA. — The trashy coin of this great empire deserves notice only by way of recreation. In 1842, we quoted the *cash* (tong-tsien) at 800 to the Spanish dollar; in 1847, the equivalent varied from 1200 to 1300, — so hard is it to fasten a value upon that which is valueless. A carpenter or tailor, we are told, receives 160 of them (say thirteen cents) for a day's work; of which sixty are required for the daily bread. The coin is extremely convenient for alms-giving, a single piece being the usual quietus for a beggar.

ECUADOR. — The quarter-dollar, or two-real piece, 1847, weighs 104, and is only 675 fine; value 18.9 cents. This depreciation corresponds with what was before noticed in some of the fractional coins of Peru.

FRANCE. — The twenty and five franc pieces of the Republic, although entirely changed in face, are the same for weight and fineness as before.

GERMANY. — Here there is no change of standards, but we observe the denomination of double-gulden, not noticed in the Manual, value 79 cents. The whole German issue of the gulden series gives an average of 900 fine by actual assay.

Since the adoption of the new rate of charges at this Mint, the thaler of Northern Germany, 750 fine, yields a return of 67¼ to 68¼ cents, according to wear; the crown, 875 fine, 106 to 107 cents.

HAYTI. — Large quantities of Haytian coins have been recoined here. They are so variable in weight and finenesss, that it is not easy to put a definite valuation upon them. They should, however, yield 76 to 78 cents per ounce, taken promiscuously, and unwashed. The piece of 100 centimes, dignified with the name of dollar, bearing the head of President Boyer, is worth about 25 cents upon an average; while that of 25 centimes, both of Petion and Boyer, averages 7½ cents. In a large promiscuous deposit of all sizes, we found the average net value of the "dollar" to be 25.7 cents. The coins range from 600 to 625 fine, if free from counterfeits, — a baser quality than is to be found in any other coinage on this side of the Atlantic. But since August, 1849, there has been a new order of things; and coin-collectors and assayers are looking with impatience for the head of Faustin the First.

MEXICO. — In 1842, we averaged recent dollars at 416½ grains, 898 fine, value 100.6 cents. The average fineness has since improved to 899, and value 100.75 cents.

The coins of two new mints have recently been tried. The doubloon of Guadalupe y Calvo, in the State of Durango, 1847, varies in weight from 417 to 420; fineness 869 to 873; average value $ 15.69. The dollar of the same mint, 1844 – 1847, averages in weight 420½, in fineness 908, and therefore in value as high as 102.8 cents. This mint began operations in 1844; its distinctive mark is G C, in the usual place in the legend.

The dollar of Culiacan, in Sinaloa, 1846 – 1848, averages 415½ grains, with a pretty wide variation in individual pieces; fineness 903; value 101 cents. The mint-mark is the letter C.

Mexican dollars are not flowing so abundantly in this direction as in former years, although they are yielding a better return.

MILAN. — The revolution of 1848 produced a new gold coin in Lombardy: it bears on the obverse a female figure with the legend, ITALIA LIBERA, DIO LO VUOLE, — "Italy free, God wills it"; and on the reverse, a wreath, within which is the denomination, 20 LIRE ITALIANE, — "20 Italian livres"; and outside of it the legend, GOVERNO PROVISORIO DI LOMBARDIA. It weighs the same as the twenty-franc piece of France, and was evidently meant as a return to the Milanese standard of 1805. The coin is more rare than could be wished: only a single specimen has reached us. Coin-collectors will consider it as a prize, for its singular beauty, and its scarcity; and as the monument of a great event in history.

NETHERLANDS. — The new 2½-guilders piece was announced in our Manual as having been decreed, but had not then been received. The legal standards are, 25 grammes (385.8 grains) in weight, 945 thousandths in fineness. The actual results of dates 1842 – 1845 are, 386 grains, 944 fine; value 98.2 cents. The coin often appears here in mixed deposits. It is remarkable for its high grade of fineness; yet it is really a depreciated issue, since, to be equal to the former guilder series, it ought to be worth 100.2 cents.

NEW GRANADA. — This country continues to send a large supply of doubloons to our market; and this makes it the more important to notice a very recent and considerable reduction in the value of the coin. Within a few months a new piece has appeared, with new devices and standards; the latter being expressed on the face of the coin by "LEI 0,900 — PESO 25,8064 G." That is, *fineness*, 900 thousandths; *weight*, so many *grammes*, — a long-drawn fraction, corresponding to 398.31 troy grains. At those rates, the piece would be worth $ 15.43,8, and would avowedly fall below the previous value of the doubloon; but upon actual trial it is still worse, as will be shown directly. This change must have taken place since the beginning of 1849, as we notice pieces of the old style bearing that date.

But as the doubloons of New Granada are alloyed almost entirely with silver, which is now profitably parted at this mint, it is necessary to restate the mint value of the older piece, as well as to give information respecting the new. The silver extracted makes a sensible addition to the values of both kinds; that is, if they are offered in sufficient quantities to meet the requirement, that the net product of a parting must be not less than five dollars; below that limit the operation is not performed.

The following terms must therefore be noticed. The doubloon of the old style, down to the early part of 1849, weighs on an average 416½ grains, and contains 870 thousandths gold, and about 120 silver; if presented in a quantity less than 58 ounces, its net mint value will be $ 15.61 ; in a larger quantity than that, it will be $ 15.66. The new doubloon, beginning with 1849, weighs 398 grains, and contains in parcels 893½ to 895 thousandths gold, say 894, and of silver about 100 ; net mint value, in any quantity less than 93 ounces, $ 15.31 ; in a larger quantity, $ 15.36.*

NORWAY. — The immigration from this country brings us considerable parcels of Norwegian and Swedish silver coins. The *dalers* of these two realms, which have the same monarch, were stated in the Manual to be interchangeable as to value, although very different as to their standards. Under our new mint charges there is some variation of value, since those of Sweden are of so much lower fineness, and are subjected to a greater charge for refining. They will be noticed in place. The daler, and half, of Norway, average 878 fine (the law calling for only 875, or seven eighths), and their weights, unworn, are respectively 446 and 223 grains; net mint value of the daler, 105 cents; the half, 52½. This valuation is down to 1848, the latest date we have seen.

PERU. — A new half-dollar, with the word PASCO in the legend, 1844, gives an average weight of 203 (variation 200 to 210), fineness 906; value 49½ cents.

PRUSSIA. — The years 1848, 1849, in other respects unsettled, show no change in the gold coinage. It still maintains its superiority to the other classes of ten and five-thaler pieces. The double-Frederick or ten-thaler, is 903 fine, weighs 206 grains, and is worth $ 8.01 ; practically, an even eight-dollar piece for us.

RUSSIA. — Five-rouble pieces of 1848 - 1849 show the fineness of 916½ ; a proof that the assaying and alloying are conducted with admirable exactness, the standard being 916⅔. The coin is worth $ 3.96,7. As the Russian mint depends, no doubt, upon the Russian mines, and not upon foreign coins, for its material, we felt an interest in examining as to what proportion of *silver* was left in the alloy of the coin, and found only 5½ thousandths. Hitherto we have found no gold coins so nearly desilvered.

SIAM. — We were not sufficiently acquainted with the silver bullets of Siam, to take account of them in the Manual. Some specimens of this curious money have since been examined. They are of different calibres, and tolerably well proportioned to each other. The *tical* weighs, without much variation, 235 grains, and is 928 fine ; value, 58.7 cents. The *salung*, 61 grains, 929 fine, 15.2 cents. The *prang*, 30 grains, 907 fine, 7.3 cents. Below this we have, as a present to the mint collection, three varieties, weighing 10, 4, and 1½ grains ; the last being worth about

* This piece is considerably reduced in diameter, as compared with the old, and is a much neater coin. The dies are apparently of English make, and the head of Liberty, which is in good flesh, greatly resembles that of the British Queen. Collectors of Roman coins will be pleasantly reminded of the *nummi victoriati.*

three eighths of a cent, and very good silver withal. A sight of it would reconcile our people to the gold dollar. Siam may claim the merit of originality in the shape of her coin, which will not admit of piling, and scarcely of lying still; the lively emblem of a true circulating medium.

SWEDEN. — The specie daler of Oscar, 1847 – 1848, is 750 fine, weighs 525 grains, and yields 104.2 cents after mint charges.

TURKEY. — There was a new system of coinage promulgated in 1840, which is noticed in our work; there is a still newer, beginning with 1845. The gold coins are evidently designed to be 22 carats (916.6) fine, as in the neighboring empire of Russia. By actual assay they are 915 fine; the piece of 100 piastres weighs 111 grains, and is worth $4.37,4; the piece of 50 piastres, 55½ grains, worth $2.18,7. In respect to value they compare with the former series of 20, 10, and 5 piastres; though entirely of different standards.

The silver coins are greatly improved in quality, and apparently based upon the Austrian standard of five sixths (833⅓) fine. They are the piece of 20 piastres, 371½ grains, 828 fine, net value 82 cents; 10 piastres, 186 grains, 826 fine, 41 cents; and 5 piastres, 92½ grains, 824 fine, 20¼ cents. These coins are well adjusted in weight, and altogether show in their way a great advance in the progress of Turkish civilization. The piastre of commerce seems to be based upon the gold; the exchange in 1845, when these coins were received, rated the piastre at 4.3 cents.

UNITED STATES. — By the law of March 3, 1849, two new gold coins, the double-eagle and the dollar, were added to the list; the former weighing 516 grains, or 21½ pennyweights, the latter $25\frac{8}{10}$ grains; and both of the fineness of nine tenths, as the other coinage. A very large number, in both denominations, have been issued.

The new postage law of March 3, 1851, provided for the coinage of a three-cent piece, composed of three fourths silver and one fourth copper, and weighing 12⅜ grains.

There are several classes of gold coin, which are not of the United States, but are struck within the national boundaries, and which ought to be noticed in this place. These are the BECHTLER'S coins of *North Carolina*, and the various *California* coins. In the same connection, it will be proper to give some details respecting several varieties of stamped ingots.

The coins of C. Bechtler are fully described in the Manual (page 160); but since the date of that publication, the mint has passed into the hands of A. Bechtler, as appears on the face of the coin; and there is a marked difference of value between the *C* and *A*. The five-dollar pieces of the former were deficient from one to six per cent. upon the the alleged value, averaging three per cent., or $4.85; the one-dollar pieces were worth 95½ to 97 cents. The five-dollar pieces of the latter vary, from the full alleged value, to a deficit of one and a half per cent. There are no dates on the coins to enable us to mark the difference; but the pieces assayed in 1843 were better than those (apparently fresh) assayed in 1849. The last and newest lot gave $4.94 to the five-dollar piece. It is to be borne in mind, that, as Bechtler's pieces are alloyed with silver, they will produce about a half of one per cent. more, if offered in sufficient quantity. The dollars, as far as tried, are two per cent. below their nominal value. The coin appears to be considerable in amount, but it is not current in the Middle and Northern States; it is frequently brought to the mint for recoinage.

The number of private mints which have been in operation in California, as indicated by specimens received here, is fourteen. Some of these have issued but a single denomination of coin, others two, and one (the Mormon) four. Besides these, there are the stamped ingots of Moffatt and Co., and of F. D. Kohler, State Assayer; and, lastly, the coin of Augustus Humbert, a United States Assayer under a legal provision of 1850.

1. The coin of "N. G. & N." does not profess the same degree of accuracy as Bechtler's, as to fineness. Its claim to be FULL WEIGHT OF HALF EAGLE is proved by a number of trials, the variation not exceeding one grain in any case; but the legend on the reverse, CALIFORNIA GOLD WITHOUT ALLOY, allows a pretty wide range. As far as our assays go, the truth of this stamp is proved; there is no alloy other than that already introduced by the hand of nature, and which is generally more than sufficient. Three pieces gave severally the fineness of 870, 880, and 892 thousandths; all were within the scope of "California gold." They consequently are worth $4.83, $4.89, and $4.95½ respectively, without the silver; and including that, 2½ cents more.

The coin is neatly executed, and, besides the two legends above quoted, bears an eagle, a circle of stars, the date 1849, and the name SAN FRANCISCO. It wears the somewhat brassy tint which belongs to gold alloyed with silver only. (See fig. 1.)

2. The mint of the "Oregon Exchange Company" issues two denominations, ten and five dollars. They respectively profess 260 and 130 grains weight of "native gold." One five-dollar piece was found to weigh 127½ grains, was 878 thousandths fine, and contained only the natural alloy: resulting value, $4.82; with the silver (in sufficiently large lots), 2½ cents more.

The coin is not well struck, but is pleasantly distinguished by the picture of a beaver, a good emblem of mining industry and of Western life. (Figures 2, 3.)

3. Next is the mintage of the "Miners' Bank, San Francisco"; a ten-dollar piece, of plain appearance.

The average weight is 263½ grains, the fineness about 865 thousandths, part of the alloy being copper. Average value $9.87, with a risk of having it as low as $9.75. (Fig. 4.)

4. Coinage of Moffatt and Co., 1849, 1850; pieces of ten and five dollars, in imitation of the national coinage. Several of the coining establishments, as will be seen, have adopted the same device, but evidently without evil intent, as most of their coins are worth what is professed, and some even more. The fineness, however, is in every case inferior to the standard of the mint, and this is likely to prove a source of discredit from European assayers, who will not take the trouble to assort. A large promiscuous lot of both kinds of Moffatt and Co.'s coins, dates

1849, 1850, shows an average of 897; average weight, to the ten-dollar piece, 258¼ grains; average value $ 9.97,7. (Figs. 5, 6.)

The S. M. V. on this and other coins is said to mean "Standard Mint Value."

5. Ten-dollar piece of J. S. O. (said to be Dr. Ormsby of Pennsylvania); one piece assayed gave 842 fine; weight 258½ grains; value $ 9.37. Very few have come to hand. (Fig. 7.)

6. Twenty-five dollar and ten-dollar pieces of Templeton Reid; weights respectively 649 and 260 grains. Being the only two specimens received, they have not been cut for assay, but appear to be of California gold without artificial alloy. Assuming this, the values would be about $ 24.50 for the first, and $ 9.75 for the second. (Figs. 8, 9.)

7. Ten-dollar and five-dollar pieces of the "Cincinnati Mining and Trading Company," 1849. These also have not been cut, on account of their rarity, but appear to be of native gold, and, at the weights of 258 and 132 grains, may be rated at $ 9.70 and $ 4.95 respectively. (Figs. 13, 14.)

8. Ten and five-dollar pieces of the "Pacific Company," 1849; very irregular in weight, and debased in fineness; a ten-dollar piece weighed 229 grains, a five-dollar, 130; assay of a third, 797 thousandths. At those rates, the larger piece would be worth $ 7.86, the smaller $ 4.48; but the valuation is altogether uncertain. (Figs. 10, 11.)

9. Five-dollar piece of the "Massachusetts and California Company," 1849; a very pretty coin, but apparently debased with copper. Only one specimen has been noticed here; it weighs 115½ grains; has not been assayed. (Fig. 12.)

10. Coins of Baldwin and Co., four varieties; 1. a ten-dollar piece, 1850, distinguished by a horse and his rider, with a lasso; 2. twenty-dollar piece; 3. ten-dollar, 1851; 4. five-dollar, 1850; the last two in imitation of United States coinage. Of the first, one piece tried weighed 263 grains, fineness 880, value $ 9.96. Of the second, four pieces tried varied from 511 to 523 grains; but one hundred pieces averaged 517; the fineness varied from 861 to 871; average fineness 868½, average value $ 19.33. Of the third, ten pieces averaged 259½ grains; average fineness 870; average value $ 9.72. Of the fourth, average value $ 4.92. (Figs. 15, 16, 17, 18.) The Baldwin coins contain some copper; about 20 thousandths.

11. Ten and five-dollar pieces of Dubosq and Co., 1850, also in imitation of the national coinage. The larger piece averages 262 grains, and three specimens gave the fineness of 899½, which is a mere shade below standard; consequent value, $ 10.15. A single five-dollar piece yielded $ 4.92. But a mixed parcel, counting $ 1,000, gave the fineness of 887, and the close value of $ 1,000.20. Consequently the pieces may be averaged at par. (Figs. 19, 20.)

12. Five-dollar piece of Shultz and Co., 1851. Average weight, 128¾ grains; fineness of three pieces, 879; value, $ 4.97.4. The devices are in imitation of United States coin. (Fig. 21.)

13. The Mormon coinage, although executed in the Territory of Utah, is without impropriety classed amongst California coins, on account

of neighborhood, and the source whence the material is derived. These are the four denominations of twenty, ten, five, and two-and-a-half dollars. Although there is much irregularity both in weight and fineness, the denominations are tolerably in proportion to each other. A parcel made up of all sizes, and counting $ 562.50, yielded at the mint $ 479.20 ; say $ 8.52 to the ten-dollar piece. The fineness was 886. (Figs. 22, 23, 24, 25.)

14. Five-dollar piece of Dunbar and Co., in imitation of United States coin. A lot of 111 pieces averages 131 grains weight, 883 fineness, value $ 4.98. (Fig. 26.)

15. Fifty-dollar piece of the United States Assay-Office at San Francisco, established by act of Congress of 1850. It first appeared here in April, 1851. The coin is prepared and issued by Messrs. Moffatt & Co. as contractors, and bears the stamp of Augustus Humbert, assayer. The two professed rates of fineness, 880 and 887 thousandths, are found upon assay here to be duly maintained, whether in single pieces or in large quantities. But some irregularity in the weight of so heavy a piece, alloyed with silver only, and offering eight corners to wear, is to be expected. When presented in quantities sufficient to allow for parting the silver, say 70 ounces, the average mint value is about $ 50.10 ; in less quantities, the silver not being allowed for, the average value is about $ 49.90. But even without the silver they occasionally come up fully to the alleged value. This coinage is understood to have put a stop to all private issues in California.

The foregoing comprehend all the varieties of *coin* that have been brought to this mint. There have been, besides, two sorts of stamped bars or ingots, evidently intended for currency.

1. The ingots of Moffatt & Co., of various sizes, from about $ 9 to $ 260. (See figures 28, 29.) It may be stated, in general, that some were found to be rated too high, and others too low. The sixteen-dollar ingot yields about $ 15.75, but is irregular.

2. The issue of bars by F. D. Kohler, Assayer of the State of California, commenced in May, 1850. (See figure 30.) They are of various sizes, from about 40 to 150 dollars. We find a slight undervaluing in his basis of calculation, and generally an error of assay in the same direction ; so that on the average his bars are worth at the mint one per cent., perhaps one and a half, more than the value stamped upon them.

II. — Recent Counterfeit Coins.

The great majority of counterfeits, new or old, deserve neither to be admired nor feared; and the fact of their obtaining any circulation proves folly on the one party, as much as roguery upon the other.

With this wholesale judgment, we dismiss a multitude of awkward Mexican birds, laughable heads of Liberty, type-metal casts, and villanous compounds of German silver; all of which are too much kept in countenance by the lingering presence in our circulation of the ugly and worn-out coin of Spanish monarchs. There are two or three varieties, however, recently brought to our notice, which deserve a more respectful attention; and these are counterfeits of gold coin only.

1. First may be mentioned, an imitation of the well-known doubloon of Bogota, in New Granada; very well executed as to appearance, but still more respectable on account of the liberal proportion of the right metal. The specimen tried here, of the date 1843, contained 653 thousandths of gold, the remainder being nearly all silver; and the weight being 416 grains, or only a half-grain below the average of the true coin: its value was $ 11.70. The value of the genuine being (irrespective of silver) about $ 15.61, the amount of profit and loss is apparent. The operators needed some advice, which an honest person would not like to give. The piece was detected by its wanting the true color, which, in such an alloy, no art of pickling can impart. Those who deal in patriot doubloons have to beware of pieces looking too pale, or too much like fine gold. In this case, the grand test of *weight* was fallacious.

2. A much more important counterfeit, or class of counterfeits, to us, is the imitation of our gold coin, lately brought to light; and which is as interesting to the man of science as it is dangerous to the commercial dealer. The varieties include the eagle, half-eagle, and quarter-eagle; there is not much danger of a false gold dollar of that manufacture, for reasons which will be obvious in the examination.

These various counterfeits began to make their appearance in 1847, although some of them bear earlier dates; and they perfectly agree in character. They are of so perfect execution, that strong apprehension was at first entertained of the surreptitious procurement of genuine dies, notwithstanding all precaution in that matter. However, upon a minute inspection, the impression, although entirely "brought up," is not so sharp and decided as in the genuine coin, and from that circumstance they have exteriorly a family character by which a practised eye may perhaps single them out. The details of impression correspond to those of the genuine, to the last microscopic particular. The most skilful and deliberate artist in the world could not take up the graver and make such a fac-simile; their dies must have been transferred from our coin by a mechanical process.

The coins have rather a dull sound in ringing, but not as if flawed; although they are actually each in three distinct pieces of metal. Some few of them, where the weight is kept up, are thicker than the genuine, and necessarily so; but generally the half-eagles run, as in the good pieces, from 55 to 60 thousandths of an inch, within the raised rim. The diameter is sometimes rather too great. The composition is as follows. A thin planchet of silver (of Spanish standard, as we found by assay) is prepared, so nearly of the right diameter that the subsequent overlaying of the gold plate at the edge will make it exact. Two other planchets, of gold, whose quality will be stated directly, are also prepared; one of them is of the right diameter of the projected coin, the other is about a quarter of an inch larger in diameter. Here are the three pieces which make up the coin. The two gold plates are then soldered upon the silver, the projecting rim of the larger disk of gold is bent up to meet the smaller, and to constitute the edge of the coin, and then the whole is finished by a blow in a coining-press. The suggestion that the coin may have been perfected in an electrotype battery is disproved by several considerations, especially by the conclusive one, that the effects of the *blow* are visible upon the silver planchet, when the gold is lifted off; and the process of *sawing out* a good coin, so as to make use of its two faces to cover a piece of silver, could not have been employed in this case, because the edge of the coin actually appertains to one of the gold surfaces; and besides, the gold is sometimes of a higher fineness than our standard.*

The eagle, of which we have had but one sample, was not particularly noted, as it came after some others of the lower denominations.

Of the half-eagle counterfeits, we have had the dates of 1844, 1845, and 1847. Of the quarter-eagle, only the date of 1843 has been shown, and this had the mint-mark, O, of the branch at New Orleans.

The half-eagle of 1844 weighed 129 grains, just the right weight; the golden part weighed 84½ grains, and was 915 thousandths (about British standard) fine; value of the gold $ 3.30. The silver weighed 44 grains, was 897 thousandths fine, and worth 10 cents; whole value of the piece, $ 3.40. Another piece, 1845, was 10 grains light; another of the same date, of which only a part was furnished, gave the assay of 902¼ thousandths for the gold on the head side, and 901¼ on the eagle side; both higher than our limit, but very near it. Two other pieces, 1847, were each about 13 grains light; specific gravity of one of them, 14.1. (That of the true coin is 17.2 to 17.5.)

Of the quarter-eagle, no less than five were offered in a single deposit for recoinage; they were severally from one to nine grains light. One piece, however, from another source, was a little over weight; the specific gravity, 12.83; fineness of the gold, 915; value of the whole piece about $ 1.25.

It only remains to inquire how these counterfeits are to be detected and avoided. First, it may be said, that to lay down any rules which

* This counterfeit is knowingly accounted for in a late newspaper paragraph. The writer says, — " The dies, under the present rules (at the United States Mint) are all pressed; hence the ease with which they can be counterfeited by any die-sinker. In England and France, the most eminent men in that branch are selected to coin dies, and such is the sharpness and perfection of their dies, that counterfeits are almost an impossibility." It was from the mints of England and France that we borrowed the improvement of transferring dies.

would protect the careless and indifferent is out of the question. Any man who can afford to take a half or quarter-eagle from any but an undoubted source, without *some* attention, can at any rate afford to be cheated out of half its value. And yet the best test we can propose is altogether an inconvenient one to any but a bank, broker, or shopkeeper. That test is *the weight.* In every case except one, which has come under our notice, the balance would have settled all doubts. An error of a grain, in an unworn piece, would be conclusive; even worn pieces of our gold coinage are never deficient, on that account, more than one grain and a half. If the counterfeit should happen to be of right weight, then its too great *thickness* would be apparent to a careful examiner.

As the balance is not a very portable or ready apparatus, several instruments have been contrived expressly for the purpose of trying gold coins, upon the principle of combining the tests of weight and dimensions. They are no doubt worth examining.

On the whole, it is difficult to say how far the appearance of this class of counterfeits should alarm the public, and make them shy of a gold currency. It is certainly the most dangerous imitation that has come to our knowledge. Yet, when it is considered that in each counterfeit of the half-eagle there is and must be from three to three and a half dollars' worth of precious metal; that the manufacture must require a good deal of machinery, and consummate skill, both artistic and mechanical; that the investment of a considerable capital is requisite, as also a wide organization for pushing the issues quietly into circulation, it may be hoped that prudent and competent persons will find it better worth their while to pursue a more honest and honorable calling. The public have an additional security, in respect to gold coins, that they are constantly passing through the various treasuries of government, the banks, and the brokers' offices, by whose vigilance that currency is kept nearly or quite pure.

We have also seen counterfeit half-eagles of the Dahlonega mint (D), of brass gilt, pretty well executed, but very light; date 1843. Also a quarter-eagle, 1846, no mint mark, copper and silver, heavily gilt; well looking, but weighing 48 grains instead of 64½.

III. — Gold from California.

In the work to which this is a supplement, information was given respecting gold bullion, in its various forms, from all the localities whence it came to this mint, including almost all the mining regions in the world then known. Since that time, the mines of California have disclosed their unrivalled treasures, and presented a new and abundant stock to operate upon. The history of this discovery and of its progress reaches the public through every newspaper, and needs no recapitulation here; but whatever is known to us as assayers, respecting this gold, will now be concisely stated.

Gold from California.

We have had opportunities of examining the auriferous product of that country in four forms: first, the superficial dirt and gravel, as it comes up by pick and spade; next, the ferruginous black sand, remaining after the earthy matter had been washed out, but containing the gold; thirdly, the vein-gold, or auriferous quartz rock; lastly (which is the appropriate work of the office), the clean gold itself, either in grains, amalgam, bars, or coins.

The first sample of *ore* was sent us by an officer in the army, during the Mexican war, and in advance of the wonderful rumors; but so perfectly exempt was this considerable invoice of stones from any thing like precious metal, that we might be forgiven for having joined in the general incredulity by which so many have been deceived, and some belated. Other specimens have since been forwarded for examination by the Hon. Secretary of the Interior, most of which were equally unproductive; disproving at least the common impression, that every thing in the gold region is a gangue for gold. One of these, a serpentine rock, contained nothing; another, the slate on which the gold deposits lie, was also free from gold; a third, the usual ferruginous quartz of mining districts, showed only a trace; while a fourth, the deposit of gravelly earth found in the bed or on the margin of a stream, yielded, upon various experiments, at the rates of ten to thirty dollars per bushel, or hundred pounds. (The amount taken at each trial was one kilogramme, over two pounds.)

The most available mode of working was found to be the ordinary one of *washing*, with some aid, at the close, from amalgamation. With a moderate degree of care, washing secures all the gold in the matrix, or brings it into a narrow and manageable compass, for recovery. To prove this, several successive trials were made of the same quantum of earth. All that remained, after the first washing, was found to be of scarcely appreciable amount; as, for instance, when the quantity first extracted was about fifteen grains, the residue afterwards obtained was only one twentieth of a grain. It is not as in our Atlantic mines, where the gold is disseminated in pyritous ores, and often in an invisible powder; where there is a wide difference between the various "yields" of washing, amalgamating, and smelting, and a still wider, between the results obtained in an analyst's laboratory, and those in extended, practical operations. Judging from experiments here, the same cannot be said of the California mining region. What is lost there, is probably not in the washing, but in the subsequent separation of the gold from the *black sand*.

What we have to say respecting the examination and treatment of the black iron sand, was laid before the public in a report to the Hon. Secretary of War. The following is an extract: —

In this last place, we have to mention an examination of some samples of sand, interspersed with gold, also forwarded by the War Department. Of this there were two parcels. The first, weighing in all about 8½ pennyweights, was first reduced in bulk by removing the grains of magnetic iron, and then subjected to cupellation, a smelting in the small way. The result of the whole treatment was as follows: —

Gold from California.

Gold, ...	9.8	parts in a thousand.		
Silver combined with gold, ...	1.2	"	"	"
Protoxide of iron (magnetic), ...	597.2	"	"	"
Residue, consisting chiefly of peroxide of iron, . .	391.8	"	"	"
	1000.0			

This would be 68.75 grains fine gold, or 77.07 grains of gold of native fineness, in a pound avoirdupois of the sand.

The other parcel was treated in two ways, both differing from the former. First, we took a specific quantity, weighed by milligrammes (equal to about 11½ pennyweights), and having cleansed it by the magnet, subjected the remainder to a very thorough amalgamation. The amount of fine gold obtained was 12.44 per thousand. Again, the same quantity of sand was thoroughly washed (more time being taken to it than would be likely to pay in a large operation), and there resulted 12.05 parts of fine gold per thousand. To give cupellation its due credit, we must remark that this second parcel was evidently the richest to the eye. The specific gravity of the black sand, without the gold, is 4.4, nearly the same as that of simple magnetic iron.

Thirdly, we have had here for examination one lot of specimens, weighing in all about 470 pounds, stated to be from the Mariposa mining district, and a fair sample of a mining vein. It was ferruginous and white quartz, very variously interspersed with gold, from a proportion entirely too small to be worth working, up to seventy dollars a pound. This is altogether characteristic of a gold mining region. An assay of some of this gold showed the high fineness of 948 thousandths. Lastly, it will interest all parties concerned to have some particulars about the gold, after it is recovered from yellow earth and black sand, and put up in merchantable shape. It comes here in four forms, as already named. Two of these, *bars* and *coins*, have been discussed under a former head; of a third, namely, *amalgam*, we have occasional deposits; and nothing need be added to what was said of that form of bullion in the Manual of Coins (page 153); the fourth, *lumps and grains* (not *dust*), is the principal condition of California gold in the market.

Those grains appear in every variety of form and size, from the shapeless lump to the beautiful oval spangle; from the weight of several pounds to the fraction of a grain; though none are so comminuted as the fine particles of African or Colombian dust. The largest lump exhibited here, thus far, weighed 265½ ounces, and was worth $ 3,900. The amorphous lumps are understood to be from the "dry diggings"; the flat spangles, and larger laminations, which show the action of running water in the rounding of their corners, are from the beds or margins of mountain streams, discharging into the two main rivers, Sacramento and San Joaquin.

As it respects any characteristic difference in the *fineness* of thegold of different locations (a very important inquiry), we have to say, that, having tried samples from various sections of the gold region, selected and marked with that view, we are unable to find any such difference. As a general rule, the flat spangles of the rivers are better than the average of other grains, perhaps as much as one per cent.; while the large lumps appear to be higher, generally, than either; not invariably, because some lots of such lumps came out unexpectedly low. The extreme boundaries of fineness of all California gold, so far, are 714 to

957; but these are so wide of the customary limits that dealers need not fear the one, nor hope for the other. The usual range is from 860 to 900. There is, however, a variety of peculiar grain, first observed here in June, 1850, which runs from 825 to 855; the alloy being, as in the other case, all silver, or nearly so. These figures refer of course to the gold after melting. In that operation there is a loss, which seems to grow each year more variable and uncertain, though progressively on the increase. In our former publication, this loss was averaged at 2½ per cent., "owing mainly to the presence of the oxide of iron which covers and penetrates every grain." It was also stated, that "if the gold grains should be dampened, or saturated with water, as is frequently their condition on opening at the mint, the loss in melting may reach four per cent." But the character of the gold in market, for some time past, is for the most part materially changed; that is, it contains more dirt and black sand. The amount of these foreign substances is well indicated in a tabular statement found in the *Alta Californian*, a daily paper of San Francisco, of March 4, 1851, containing the actual results of meltings at the United States Assay Office of California, by which it appears that they find a variation of loss, from two to eleven per cent.; the average being about six per cent. This corresponds with the experience of the mint. Amalgamated gold loses five to seven per cent., averaging the same as the grains. The average value of the gold in grains or amalgam, as indicated by a recent estimate, is $ 17.25 per ounce; the range being from $ 16.25 to $ 18.25. The allowance for silver parted, when a sufficient quantity of gold is presented in one item, say fifty to eighty ounces, according to quality, makes an increase of value of six or eight cents per ounce.

The gold of California sometimes contains a little platinum, but more frequently the osmiuret of iridium, in quantities too minute to affect the value, but sufficient to require watching, in mint operations. The alloy of the gold ordinarily is silver, with a little iron. It is the coating of the oxide of iron which gives the gold its rich hue, almost resembling that of fine gold. As that is removed in melting, the metal comes out so much paler than before, that persons unacquainted with the matter might suspect a wilful admixture of silver. The people of California understand this, from the comparison of bars and coins made there with the native grains.

The manufacture of mammoth lumps has been carried on to some extent in California, and apparently for different purposes. At first, the genuine California gold, being taken fluid from the melting-pot, was ingeniously mingled with broken bits of quartz, producing a specimen which at once astonished the beholder, and commanded an extra price. But this was legerdemain of the golden age. They have since found a method of imposing upon traders with a base mixture, about half gold, the rest silver and copper; which, being cast out amongst stones, and afterwards pickled, certainly presents quite a *native* appearance, very likely to deceive. Several such have been offered at the mint. They can always be detected, however, by one of the surfaces (the bottom one) showing marks of previous fusion. A little cutting, also, soon betrays the hardness and redness.

IV. — Recapitulation of the net Mint Value of Gold and Silver Coins, issued within Twenty-five Years past.

N. B. Inquiry has been frequently made at the mint for a compend of the values of foreign coins, without a due consideration of the difficulty of putting in a small space such a statement as would be satisfactory. The quarto volume, to which this is supplementary, was not found too large for its purpose, which was to supply such information as dealers, amateurs, and legislators would from time to time be likely to require. Still, a condensed table of the coins more usually seen, and within a contracted range of date, would certainly be useful to dealers and others, and especially with the modifications occasioned by the new mint tariff of charges. We therefore offer the following, inserting values only, and leaving the details of legal weight and fineness, and of actual weight and fineness, to be sought for in the larger work; as also the particulars concerning coinage of older date than just specified.

Gold Coins.

		D. C. M.
Austria.	Quadruple ducat,	9.12
	Ducat,	2.27 5
	Sovereign (for Lombardy),	6.75
Baden,	Five Gulden,	2.04
Bavaria.	Ducat,	2.27
Belgium.	Twenty-franc piece,	3.83 2
	Twenty-five-franc piece,	4.72
Bolivia.	Doubloon,	15.58
Brazil.	Piece of 6,400 reis,	8.72
Britain.	Sovereign,	4.84 5
Brunswick.	Ten thaler,	7.89
California.	See *United States.*	
Central America.	Doubloon,	14.96
	Escudo,	1.67
Costa Rica.	Half-doubloon, 1850,	7.62
Chili.	Doubloon (before 1835),	15.57
	" (1835 and since),	15.66
Denmark.	Double Fred., or Ten-thaler,	7.88
Ecuador.	Half-doubloon,	7.60
Egypt.	Hundred piastres	4.97
France.	Twenty francs,	3.85
Greece.	Twenty drachms,	3.45
Hanover.	Ten-thaler, George IV.,	7.84
	Do. Wm. IV. and Ernest,	7.89
Hindustan.	Mohur, E. I. Company,	7.10
Mecklenburg.	Ten-thaler,	7.89
Mexico.	Doubloon, average,	15.53
Netherlands.	Ducat,	2.26 5
	Ten guilders,	4.00 7
New Granada.	Doubloon, 21 carat std.,	15.61
	" includ. the silver,	15.66
	" nine tenths std.,	15.31
	" includ. the silver,	15.36
Persia.	Tomaun,	2.23
Peru.	Doubloon, Lima, to 1833,	15.55
	" Cuzco, to 1833,	15.62
	" " 1837,	15.53

Gold Coins.

		D. C. M.
Portugal.	Half-joe (full weight),	8.65
	Crown,	5.81
Prussia.	Double Frederick,	8.00
Rome.	Ten scudi,	10.37
Russia.	Five roubles,	3.96 7
Sardinia.	Twenty lire,	3.84 5
Saxony.	Ten-thaler,	7.94
	Ducat,	2.26
Spain.	Pistole (quarter-doubloon),	3.90 5
Turkey.	Hundred piastres,	4.37 4
	Twenty piastres (new),	82
Tuscany.	Sequin,	2.30
U. States.	Eagle (before June, 1834),	10.62
	Five-dollar piece of C. Bechtler, average,	4.85
	Dollar of the same, average,	96
	Five-dollar piece of A. Bechtler,	4.92 to 5.00
	Dollar of the same,	98
	Oregon Exch. Co., Five dollars,	4.82
	N. G. and N., San Fr., Five dollars,	4.83 to 4.95
	Miners' Bank, " Ten " average,	9.87
	Moffatt's Ten-dollar piece,	9.98
	" Five-dollar "	5.00
	" Sixteen-dollar ingot,	15.75
	J. S. O., Ten-dollar piece,	9.37
	T. Reid, Twenty-five-dollar piece,	24.50
	" Ten-dollar "	9.75
	Pacific Company, ten and five, uncertain.	
	Mass. Company, five, uncertain.	
	Cincinnati Co., ten, estimated,	9.70
	" five, "	4.95
	Baldwin, twenty dollars,	19.33
	" ten " with horseman,	9.96
	" " " second issue,	9.72
	" five " "	4.92
	Dubosq, ten "	10.00
	" five "	5.00
	Shults, " "	4.97

Mint Value of Gold and Silver Coins.

GOLD COINS.

	D. C. M.
Dunbar, five dollars, . . .	4.98
Humbert, U. S. Assayer, fifty dollars,	50.00
Mormon coinage, twenty doll., average	17.00
" ten "	8.50
" five "	4.25
" two-and-a-half doll.,	2.12

Kohler's bars, about one per cent. higher than his valuation.

SILVER COINS.

		D. C. M.
AUSTRIA.	Rix dollar, ...	97
	Florin, ...	48 5
	Twenty kreutzers, . .	16
	Lira (for Lombardy), .	16
BADEN.	Crown, ...	1.07
	Gulden or florin, . . .	39 5
BAVARIA.	Crown, ...	1.06 5
	Florin, ...	39 5
	Six kreutzers, . . .	03
BELGIUM.	Five francs, . . .	93
	Two and a half francs, .	46 5
	Two francs, . .	37
	Franc, ...	18 5
BOLIVIA.	Dollar, ...	1.00 6
	Half-dollar debased, 1830, .	37 5
	Quarter " " .	18 7
BRAZIL.	Twelve hundred reis, . .	99 2
	Eight " " . .	66
	Four " " . .	33
BREMEN.	Thirty-six grote, . .	35 6
BRITAIN.	Half-crown, ...	54
	Shilling, ...	21 7
	Fourpence, ...	07 1
BRUNSWICK.	Thaler, . . .	68
CENTRAL AMERICA.	Dollar. Uncertain; say	97
	Costa Rica, new real of,	05 8
CHILI.	Dollar, ...	1.01
	Quarter-dollar, ...	22 4
	Eighth " or real, . .	11 2
DENMARK.	Rigsbank daler, . . .	52 3
	Specie " . .	1.04 7
	Thirty-two skillings, . .	17
ECUADOR.	Quarter-dollar, . . .	18 7
EGYPT.	Twenty piastres, . . .	96
FRANCE.	Five francs, ...	93 2
	Franc, ...	18 5
FRANKFORT.	Florin, ...	39 5
GREECE.	Drachm, ...	16 5
GUIANA, British.	Guilder, . .	26 2
HANOVER.	Thaler, fine silver, . .	69 2
	" 750 fine, . .	68
HAYTI.	Dollar, or 100 centimes, . .	25 7
HESSE-CASSEL.	Thaler, . .	67 5
	One-sixth thaler, .	11
HESSE-DARMSTADT.	Florin or Gulden,	39 5
HINDUSTAN.	Rupee, ...	44 5
MEXICO.	Dollar, average, . . .	1.00 7
NAPLES.	Scudo, ...	94
NETHERLANDS.	Three guilders, .	1.20
	Guilder, . . .	40
	Twenty-five cents, .	09 5
	Two and a half guilders,	98 2
NEW GRANADA.	Dollar, usual weight,	1.02
	Dollar, or ten reals, 1851, .	93
NORWAY.	Rigsdaler, ...	1.05
PERSIA.	Sahib-koran, ...	21 5
PERU.	Dollar, Lima mint, . . .	1.00 6
	" Cuzco, . . .	1.00 8
	Half-dollar, Cuzco, debased, .	36
	" Arequipa, debased,	36
	" Pasco, . . .	49 5
POLAND.	Zloty, ...	11 2
PORTUGAL.	Cruzado, ...	55 2
	Crown, of 1000 reis, .	1.12
	Half-crown, . . .	56
PRUSSIA.	Thaler, average, . .	68
	One sixth thaler, average, .	11
	Double Thaler, or 3½ Gulden,	1.39
ROME.	Scudo, ...	1.00 5
	Teston (3-10 scudo), .	30
RUSSIA.	Rouble, ...	75
	Ten Zloty, ...	1.13 5
	Thirty copecks, . . .	22
SARDINIA.	Five lire, . . .	93 2
SAXONY.	Species-thaler, . . .	96
	Thaler (XIV. F. M.), .	68
SIAM.	Tical, ...	58 5
SPAIN.	Pistareen (4 reals vellon), .	19 5
SWEDEN.	Species-daler, ...	1.04 2
	Half " . . .	52
TURKEY.	Twenty piastres, new coinage,	82
TUSCANY.	Leopoldone, . .	1.05
	Florin, ...	26 2
WURTEMBERG.	Gulden, 1824, . .	38 5
	" 1838, and since,	39 5
	Double thaler, or 3½ Gulden,	1.39

V.—Silver from Lake Superior.

Scarcely any discovery of late date has better deserved the attention of men of science, than that of silver occurring in the copper mines of Lake Superior. Hitherto it has been produced in but small quantity; possibly the finding of a rich *pocket* may yet command the respect of business-men. The silver is in the native or metallic state, and appears in grains or lumps, firmly attached, or as it were *welded*, to the copper; and yet the two metals are not at all intermingled or alloyed. Deducting a small proportion of mere earthy matter, the silver is pure, not even containing gold; and the copper is pure also. We are not aware that silver has ever been found, elsewhere, in this most curious position.

Three deposits of this silver have already been made at the mint. One had been previously melted and cast into bars, and consequently its character was gone, though not its value. The second was a large wide-spreading *cake*, smoothed somewhat by the action of water; it was found by assay to contain ninety-five per cent. unalloyed silver, and five per cent. earthy matter. The value of it was $ 119. This has been retained in the collection of the mint, and forms one of its greatest curiosities. The third deposit, brought very recently, and emanating from the Pittsburg Company, consisted of grains or lumps, varying in weight from one grain to four pennyweights (say a quarter of a cent to a quarter of a dollar); they had been detached from the copper, and so effectually that very little of that metal remained. The amount of dirt removed by melting was about two per cent.; the remainder showed a fineness of 962 thousandths. The whole weight was about 238 ounces; and the value, $ 290.

VI.—Table of Correspondence between Pennyweights and Grains, and the Decimal Fractions of a Troy Ounce.

Gold and silver bullion, and coins in quantity, are weighed at the United States Mint and its branches by ounces and hundredths, rejecting the usual division into pennyweights and grains. It were much to be wished that this easy decimal system were brought into general use. Probably that wish will ere long be realized; but in the mean time, it is desirable for dealers and depositors to have ready means of knowing the equivalents in the two methods of weighing. The ensuing table is carried to four decimals of the ounce, instead of two, as in our former publication. The first two places show the hundredths, which the depositor requires; the two additional places go to the ten-thousandths, which are very convenient in the calculation of the value of a single coin, and for other purposes. The twentieth of a grain is thereby reached.

Table of Correspondence between Pennyweights and Grains, and the Decimal Fractions of a Troy Ounce.

	0	1	2	3	4	5	6	7	8	9	10	11	12	13	14	15	16	17	18	19	20	21	22	23
0	.0000	.0021	.0042	.0063	.0083	.0104	.0125	.0146	.0167	.0188	.0208	.0229	.0250	.0271	.0292	.0313	.0333	.0354	.0375	.0396	.0417	.0438	.0458	.0479
1	.0500	.0521	.0542	.0563	.0583	.0604	.0625	.0646	.0667	.0688	.0708	.0729	.0750	.0771	.0792	.0813	.0833	.0854	.0875	.0896	.0917	.0938	.0958	.0979
2	.1000	.1021	.1042	.1063	.1083	.1104	.1125	.1146	.1167	.1188	.1208	.1229	.1250	.1271	.1292	.1313	.1333	.1354	.1375	.1396	.1417	.1438	.1458	.1479
3	.1500	.1521	.1542	.1563	.1583	.1604	.1625	.1646	.1667	.1688	.1708	.1729	.1750	.1771	.1792	.1813	.1833	.1854	.1875	.1896	.1917	.1938	.1958	.1979
4	.2000	.2021	.2042	.2063	.2083	.2104	.2125	.2146	.2167	.2188	.2208	.2229	.2250	.2271	.2292	.2313	.2333	.2354	.2375	.2396	.2417	.2438	.2458	.2479
5	.2500	.2521	.2542	.2563	.2583	.2604	.2625	.2646	.2667	.2688	.2708	.2729	.2750	.2771	.2792	.2813	.2833	.2854	.2875	.2896	.2917	.2938	.2958	.2979
6	.3000	.3021	.3042	.3063	.3083	.3104	.3125	.3146	.3167	.3188	.3208	.3229	.3250	.3271	.3292	.3313	.3333	.3354	.3375	.3396	.3417	.3438	.3458	.3479
7	.3500	.3521	.3542	.3563	.3583	.3604	.3625	.3646	.3667	.3688	.3708	.3729	.3750	.3771	.3792	.3813	.3833	.3854	.3875	.3896	.3917	.3938	.3958	.3979
8	.4000	.4021	.4042	.4063	.4083	.4104	.4125	.4146	.4167	.4188	.4208	.4229	.4250	.4271	.4292	.4313	.4333	.4354	.4375	.4396	.4417	.4438	.4458	.4479
9	.4500	.4521	.4542	.4563	.4583	.4604	.4625	.4646	.4667	.4688	.4708	.4729	.4750	.4771	.4792	.4813	.4833	.4854	.4875	.4896	.4917	.4938	.4958	.4979
10	.5000	.5021	.5042	.5063	.5083	.5104	.5125	.5146	.5167	.5188	.5208	.5229	.5250	.5271	.5292	.5313	.5333	.5354	.5375	.5396	.5417	.5438	.5458	.5479
11	.5500	.5521	.5542	.5563	.5583	.5604	.5625	.5646	.5667	.5688	.5708	.5729	.5750	.5771	.5792	.5813	.5833	.5854	.5875	.5896	.5917	.5938	.5958	.5979
12	.6000	.6021	.6042	.6063	.6083	.6104	.6125	.6146	.6167	.6188	.6208	.6229	.6250	.6271	.6292	.6313	.6333	.6354	.6375	.6396	.6417	.6438	.6458	.6479
13	.6500	.6521	.6542	.6563	.6583	.6604	.6625	.6646	.6667	.6688	.6708	.6729	.6750	.6771	.6792	.6813	.6833	.6854	.6875	.6896	.6917	.6938	.6958	.6979
14	.7000	.7021	.7042	.7063	.7083	.7104	.7125	.7146	.7167	.7188	.7208	.7229	.7250	.7271	.7292	.7313	.7333	.7354	.7375	.7396	.7417	.7438	.7458	.7479
15	.7500	.7521	.7542	.7563	.7583	.7604	.7625	.7646	.7667	.7688	.7708	.7729	.7750	.7771	.7792	.7813	.7833	.7854	.7875	.7896	.7917	.7938	.7958	.7979
16	.8000	.8021	8042	.8063	.8083	.8104	.8125	.8146	.8167	.8188	.8208	.8229	.8250	.8271	.8292	.8313	.8333	.8354	.8375	.8396	.8417	.8438	.8458	.8479
17	.8500	.8521	.8542	.8563	.8583	.8604	.8625	.8646	.8667	.8688	.8708	.8729	.8750	.8771	.8792	.8813	.8833	.8854	.8875	.8896	.8917	.8938	.8958	.8979
18	.9000	.9021	.9042	.9063	.9083	.9104	.9125	.9146	.9167	.9188	.9208	.9229	.9250	.9271	.9292	.9313	.9333	.9354	.9375	.9396	.9417	.9438	.9458	9479
19	.9500	.9521	.9542	.9563	.9583	.9604	.9625	.9646	9667	.9688	.9708	.9729	.9750	.9771	.9792	.9813	.9833	.9854	.9875	.9896	.9917	.9938	.9958	.9979

VII.—Comparison of American and Foreign Weights used for Precious Metals.

The normal weight of this mint is the troy ounce, for considerable quantities; and the troy grain, for single coins.

This ounce is equal to 480 grains; to 31.09815 French grammes; to 1.08108 Spanish ounces.

The grain is 64.788 milligrammes.

Our standard French kilogramme weighs 15,435 grains, or 32.15625 ounces.

The gramme is 15.435 grains.

The milligramme, .0154 gr.

The average estimate of the Spanish mark is 3,552 troy grains, or 7.40 ounces troy. It is differently subdivided, according as it is applied to the weighing of gold or silver. For gold, it is divided into 50 castellanos; each castellano into 8 tomines; each tomine into 12 granos. For silver, the mark is divided into 8 ounces; each ounce into 8 ochavos; each ochavo into 6 tomines; each tomine into 12 granos. Consequently, in gold weighings there are 4,800 grains, and in silver 4,608 grains, to the mark.

The castellano is much used, however, as a normal weight for gold bullion. By deduction from the above, it should weigh 71.04 troy grains; by an invoice from New Granada, we have found it to correspond with 70.935; so that 71 grains might be taken as the equivalent, accurate enough in practice. This is just one grain less than three pennyweights; or .1479 of a troy ounce.

This mark, being employed not only in Spain, but in all Spanish America, is of course a very important weight to the bullion and coin dealer, and should be duly understood. It is perhaps not more difficult to master than the pounds troy and avoirdupois, with their respective trains.

The Cologne mark, normal money-weight of Germany, by the German Convention of 1838, was estimated at 233.855 grammes, answering to 3609.55 grains troy. It was before rated usually at 3609.

Our silver dollar, since 1837, weighs 26.725 grammes.

A kilogramme of standard ($\frac{9}{10}$) gold is worth $ 598.25,5.

VIII.—Bulk and Packing of Precious Metals.

A solid or cubic inch of fine gold weighs 10.1509 ounces, and is worth $ 209.84.

A cubic foot of the same, $ 362,600.

A cubic inch of standard gold weighs 9.0989 ounces, and is worth $ 169.28.

A cubic foot of the same, $ 292,500.

A cubic inch of fine silver weighs 5.5225 ounces, and is worth $ 7.14.

A cubic foot of the same, $ 12,338.

A cubic inch of standard silver weighs 5.4173 ounces, and is worth $ 6.30,3.

A cubic foot of the same, $ 10,891.*

Gold is not measured by the *pint*, at least out of California; yet it may be interesting to know, that a dry-measure pint of California grains is found to weigh from 141 to 143½ ounces; value about $ 2,560. The average specific gravity is consequently 9.61; so that it occupies about twice as much bulk, in that form, as when melted and cast into bars. A pint of African dust was found to weigh 148 ounces.

The advantage of having gold grains or dust cast into bars, as a preparative for exportation, is perhaps overrated. True, it has rather an insufficient outfit, if packed in paper, leather, muslin, Seidlitz-boxes, or porter-bottles, as it came at first from San Francisco. A good tin box, well soldered, will hold fast and keep dry; and the mint charges nothing for melting. This is the most general kind of packing now used; but the tin case, if large, requires to be inclosed in a wooden box, and after that there is need of a vigilant watch and care. A most daring theft was lately committed, somewhere on the route, by boring through box and case; and about $ 9,000 worth was abstracted.

A keg 13½ inches high, including the chine, and with a diameter of 10 inches at the head and 11½ at the bilge (outside measures), is a convenient size for $ 2,000 in silver coin, or $ 50,000 in gold coin.

A keg whose measurements are 19, 11, 13, as above, is a proper size for $ 5,000 in silver coin.

A rectangular box, measuring inside 10 by 8 inches by 5 in depth, is the size used at the mint for $ 1,000 in silver coin. This allows the coin to be thrown in promiscuously; if piled, at least one third more can be put in. Such a box would hold $ 36,000 in gold coin, laid in order; or $ 27,000 in disorder.

A bag 6 inches by 9 holds $ 5,000 in gold coin, with room to tie.

A bag 14 by 18 is a good size for $ 1,000 in silver coin.

One thousand pieces of our three-cent coin ($ 30 worth) make a smaller budget than many of our customers seem to anticipate. A bag 3½ inches by 5 easily contains them.

---

* The above calculations are based upon the weight of water as 252.458 grains to the cubic inch, the thermometer being at 60° and the barometer 30 inches. (Silliman's First Princ. Chem., 1848.) The specific gravity of fine gold is taken at 19.3, standard at 17.3; fine silver 10.5, standard 10.3. As these gravities are only approximate, we may be excused for not carrying out the decimals very far, as is rather too often done in works of science.

IX.—Determination of the Value of a Specimen of Gold or Silver in its Native Rock, or Gangue.

That which is as old as Archimedes may yet be new to some; that a specimen of gold or silver, as it comes from its natural bed, intermingled with stone, and often more prized for its beauty, or as a keepsake, than the metal would be in a more condensed and marketable shape, can be accurately enough valued without being broken up or spoiled. The specific gravity of the lump being determined, and that of the metal and the matrix being known, the problem is solved by a direct calculation. The formula is inserted here, as being a suitable and convenient place for it.

Let a represent the specific gravity of the metal.
" b " " " of the stone.
" c " " " of the lump.
" w " the weight of the lump.
" x " " of the gold.
" y " " of the stone.

$$\text{Then, } x = \frac{a\,(c-b)}{c\,(a-b)}\,w;$$

$$\text{and } y = \frac{b\,(a-c)}{c\,(a-b)}\,w.$$

Or, to put the rule in arithmetical form:—

1. From the specific gravity of the lump deduct the specific gravity of the quartz (say 2.63), or whatever the matrix may be.
2. Multiply the remainder by the specific gravity of the *metal*.
3. Multiply the weight of the lump by the last product, which will make a second product which we will call P.
4. From the specific gravity of the metal deduct the specific gravity of the matrix.
5. Multiply the difference by the specific gravity of the lump.
6. Take this product for a divisor, to divide the above product P; the quotient will be the weight of metal in the lump.

The only source of error is in the variableness of the specific gravity of the stony part. In the case of silver in limestone, 2.60 has been proved by our experiments to be a good basis for the matrix; in respect to gold in quartz, much depends upon whether the latter is white, or tinged with iron; compact, or loose and cellular. We have found 2.63 a good medium for all cases except that of hard white rock, where it is more accurate to take 2.65. The problem has been often and satisfacfactorily proved here by meltings; of course, not to all the nicety that analysis or arithmetic can be carried.

Where the specimen is bulky, and the stony matter predominates, a convenient way of getting the specific gravity is that given in Patterson's Arithmetic, essentially as follows:—

Provide a suitable water-tight vessel, say a pitcher or jar, that will rather more than hold the specimen, and not over-large at the opening. Fill the vessel with water, to a mark. Then pour, or draw off with a syphon, into another smaller vessel, so much of the water as will allow you freely to insert the specimen. After this, fill up to the mark again, from the water drawn off. The remainder of drawn water is exactly equal in bulk to the specimen; the weight of that water, therefore, gives the divisor; the weight of the specimen (dry), the dividend; the quotient is its specific gravity.

The value of this mode, when conducted with due care, has been satisfactorily tested here by the returns from the crucible.

X. — Transaction of Business at the Mint.

The oversight of the Mint, and to a certain extent of the Branch Mints also, is by law committed to one principal officer, named the Director, who is under the general control of the Secretary of the Treasury.

The operations of the Mint are divided into five departments; — 1. Receipt and disbursement. 2. Assaying the precious metals, including the primary melting for assay. 3. Melting and refining for coinage. 4. Coining, through all its stages. 5. Die-engraving. The first principally concerns those who have pecuniary transactions with the Mint; and its chief is styled the Treasurer.

The four offices nearest to the front door are those assigned to the Treasurer.

In the office to the left, entering, applications are to be made for the payment of bills for materials furnished, or whatever belongs to expenditure of the establishment; also for the payment of bullion deposits, and for memorandums thereof; also for the distribution of copper coins; and, generally, for information about all those matters. Persons bringing bullion should also enter at this office, where they will be directed to the counter of the next, which is the weighing-room.

In this second office the weigher receives the bullion, weighs it in presence of the depositor, records the transaction, and gives a receipt in the following form: —

No. 5,000. MINT OF THE UNITED STATES,
Philadelphia, June 1, 1851.

Received from G. Bain, a Deposit of Gold Bullion, for Coinage, weighing twelve hundred and forty-one $\frac{82}{100}$ *Ounces, the net Value thereof to be ascertained, and paid to said Depositor, or Order, in Gold Coins of the United States, agreeably to Law.*

Oz. 1,241$\frac{82}{100}$. *J. E. N., for the Treasurer.*

The deposit is then melted under the supervision of the assayer, reweighed, and assayed, without delay. By these operations, and by a subsequent double calculation based upon them, the exact mint value of the parcel is determined, to the satisfaction of the director, who thereupon issues a warrant to the treasurer for payment thereof, in coin.

Bullion or foreign coin brought to the mint in a state fit for casting into ingots for coining, is subject to no charge. In other cases, there is a deduction made from the value, according to the following tariff of charges: —

I. For Refining, when the Bullion is below standard.

1. *On Gold.* — Three cents per ounce of gross weight after melting, on so much of a deposit as will bring the whole up to standard.

2. *On Silver.* — From 500 to 700 fine, 3 cents per oz. as above.
 " 701 to 800 " 2½ " " "
 " 801 to 899 " 2 " " "
 On so much as will bring the whole up to standard.

II. For Toughening, when metals are contained in it which render it unfit for Coinage.

1. *On Gold.* — From one to three and a half cents per ounce of gross weight after melting, according to the condition of the metal.

2. *On Silver.* — If not Coppery, one third to one cent per ounce, as above.
 If Coppery, 500 to 700 fine, 3 cents per oz. as above.
 " 701 to 800 " 2½ " " "
 " 801 to 925 " 2 " " "

III. For Copper, used for Alloy, two cents per ounce.

IV. For Silver, introduced into the Alloy of Gold, one hundred and twenty-nine cents per ounce.

V. For Separating the Gold and Silver, when these metals exist together in the bullion.

1. If not Coppery:
 Proportion of Gold 1 to 200 thous. 1½ cents per oz. gross, after melting.
 " " 201 to 600 " 2 " " " "
 " " 601 to 700 " 3 " " " "
 " " 701 to 800 " 4 " " " "
 " " 801 to 935 " 5 " " " "

2. If Coppery:
 Proportion of Silver 500 to 700 fine, the Gold in any proportion not less than 1½ thousandths, ... 3 cents per oz. gross, after melting.
 Proportion of Silver 701 to 800 fine, 2½ " " " "
 " " 801 to 925 " 2 " " " "

Neither gold nor silver is separated for the benefit of the depositor, when the net product of the operation, estimated upon the above charges, shall be less than five dollars.

After a delay of three to eight days (according to the pressure of business), the depositor or his indorsee returns to the mint for payment; receives the memorandum and warrant in the first office above mentioned, and, crossing the rotunda to the pay-office, receives his money by tale, checked by weight.

The fourth office is appropriated to the assistant treasurership of the United States. It has no connection with the mint, other than being located within its walls, — a location which proves to be, in various respects, of public advantage.

XI. — Miscellanies.

1. *Shipments of California Gold to London.* — From various "accounts-sales" of California gold, shipped from San Francisco to London, it appears, that, while the charges at London are greater than here, and the bullion is paid for there at a reduction from the legal mint value,

yet the *shipping* charges, comprehending freight, commission, insurance, and brokerage, are so much less to the English ports than to our own, that the balance is thrown considerably the other way. The expenses on bullion up to the depositing at the mint amount to 5½ to 6 per cent.; while the same expenses to London (from California) are only 4 per cent. Notwithstanding this considerable inequality, the great bulk of the gold, so far, finds its way to this mint.

2. *Wear of our Silver Coins.* — Half-dollars of the old standard, previous to 1837, of average wear, are found to have lost 5¼ tenths of one per cent. A recoinage of $ 38,000 produced $ 37,800, in June, 1845.

Dimes and half-dimes of old standard (no date earlier than 1824), about equally mixed, are light by wear, six per cent.

The same, of new standard, 1837 – 50, light one and a half per cent.

3. *Gold Pens* have enough gold in them to answer their purpose, and to make them of some value when worn out. One sample gave 9½ grains, 465 thousandths fine; value, 19 cents. Another, 12 grains, 500 fine; worth 26 cents. A third, 6½ grains, 481 fine; value, 13½ cents.

4. *Georgia Diamonds.* — One of these, found in Hall County, Georgia, was shown at this mint in November, 1845. Weight, 6$\frac{8}{10}$ grains; about 2$\frac{1}{6}$ diamond carats. Specific gravity, 3.54. Sold in the rough state for forty dollars.

Another, from the same region, February, 1846, weighed nine grains.

5. *Our Copper Coinage*, to the end of 1850, amounted to $ 1,296,201. Adding to this the first quarter of 1851, $ 30,646, we have, of that ponderous currency, about 1,590 *tons*, of 2,000 pounds avoirdupois. This circulation is almost entirely confined to the Northern and Middle States, as it is rejected by the South and West.

6. *American Spoons and Stirrups.* — A lot of gold teaspoons, deposited at the mint, from the West Indies, yielded about twenty dollars to each spoon. Mexican silver stirrups, fifty dollars in the pair.

PLEDGES OF HISTORY.

A BRIEF ACCOUNT

OF THE

COLLECTION OF COINS

BELONGING TO THE

MINT OF THE UNITED STATES,

MORE PARTICULARLY OF

THE ANTIQUE SPECIMENS.

By WILLIAM E. DU BOIS.

SECOND EDITION, WITH ADDITIONS.

1851.

COLLECTION

OF

SPECIMEN COINS

AT THE MINT, PHILADELPHIA.

THE suite of apartments in the mint appropriated to the exhibition of coins, ores, and national medals occupies the front of the building in the second story, and measures sixteen feet wide by fifty-four feet long. Originally there were three rooms, connecting with each other by folding-doors; the removal of these has made one large saloon, with recesses, very commodious and suitable for the use to which it is applied. The eastern and western rooms are of uniform size and construction; the central one has a dome and skylight, supported by four columns; with a corresponding window in its floor (protected by a railing) to light the hall of entrance below.

The ancient coins are displayed in eight cases, mitred in pairs, and placed erect against the walls in the wide doorways and the middle room. The modern coins are variously arranged;. part (including all those of the United States) being in a nearly level case which surrounds the railing above mentioned; and part being in upright cases, disposed along the walls of the middle and west rooms. The ores, minerals, and metallic alloys are placed in the west room; in the eastern are shown the national and other medals, and the fine beams used for the adjustment of weights. The middle room also contains portraits of the directors of the mint, beginning with Rittenhouse, the first director. All the cases are fronted with glass, and, besides allowing an inspection of every specimen, present an agreeable *coup d'œil* on entering the room, especially by the middle door.

Visitors are admitted at prescribed hours, if attended by an officer or conductor of the institution.

The collection was commenced in June, 1838. Long before that date, however, Mr. Adam Eckfeldt, formerly chief coiner, led as well by his own taste as by the expectation that a conservatory would some day be established, took pains to preserve master-coins of the different annual issues of mint, and to retain some of the finest foreign specimens, as they appeared in deposit for recoinage. As soon as a special annual appropriation was instituted for this object by Congress (which was as soon as it was asked), the collection took a permanent form, and from the nucleus above mentioned, has gone on in a continual course of augmentation ever since. It is now nearly as large as we expect or wish to have it, excepting, however, that specimens of new coinage, domestic or foreign, must be added as they appear.

For effecting this purpose we have had singular facilities. A great majority of the coins — almost all of those not over three hundred years old — have been culled from deposits, and consequently have cost us no more than their bullion value. They are, moreover, the choicest of their kind; and perhaps there are few cabinets where so large a proportion of the pieces are in so fine preservation, as well the ancient as the modern. We have also the advantage of the correspondence and aid of gentlemen abroad, some of them officially related to our government, and all of them experienced in this business, and disposed to respond to our wishes. To specify this assistance (as it deserves), we have received from J. G. Schwarz, Esq., United States Consul at Vienna, the greater part of our ancient coins, being a private collection, the result of twenty years' assiduity; from John P. Brown, Esq., Dragoman to the United States embassy at Constantinople, we have a very considerable proportion of the same, especially Greek and Byzantine, with a series of Ottoman coins (thus far at the usual market prices); from the late Dr. Grant, connected with the American Christian mission to the Nestorians, through his son, a small number of ancient and rare Persian coins; from the honorable East India Company, a selection from the very scarce and curious antiques of Middle Asia, chiefly Greek-Bactrian, of which they have lately come in possession, and in which branch they have almost the monopoly; from C. Stokes, Esq., of London (besides his influence in procuring the parcel last mentioned), a number of scarce coins of England and the American colonies (these in a way of honorary exchange); from Dr. Huffnagle, of Calcutta, an extended series of Asiatic coins; a parcel of scarce Hindu coins was purchased of Mr. Morris, a missionary; and from several individuals, mostly of this country, we have promiscuous specimens by donation. The disposition to place curiosities of this kind in a situation where they will be the most accessible, and, it is hoped, the most stationary, is thankfully commended.

At the present time, the aggregate of specimens is about 650 in gold, 2,100 in silver, 1,200 in billon, brass, copper, &c.; in all 3,950. Of these, the ancient Greek and Roman number 82 in gold, 503 in silver, and 480 in other metals; in all, 1,065. Compared with the numismatic cabinets of Europe, our collection is indeed but a dwarf in size, and may stand second, in that respect, to some in this country. But it was not our purpose to amass an immense store of coins, the very multitude of which might deter from its examination. We are rather willing to be the first to set an example of moderation in a pursuit which has its temptations to extravagance and excess

REMARKS ON THE COINS OF THE ROMAN EMPIRE.

THE interest excited by the examination of a curious coin generally has reference to the following particulars: — I. Its country and date. II. Material, or composition. III. Denomination and value. IV. The meaning of its legends and devices. V. The style of its execution; and VI. Its present degree of rarity.

A few general explanations will here be offered on each of those points, as they relate to the coins of the Roman Empire.

I. The coins of which these are specimens were the current money of ancient Rome; an empire founded (by the usual reckoning) seven hundred and fifty-three years before Christ, and finally extinguished A. D. 1453. According to their respective places in this vast tract of time, they exemplify the rudeness and poverty of a petty colony, the grandeur of an immense dominion, and the decay and barbarism of its feeble remnants.

When we come to display these relics in their historical order, only one considerable difficulty is presented. We know, indeed, that the rough pieces of base metal were the earliest currency of Rome, sufficient for a poor and warlike horde. The pieces of silver, bearing only the insignia and name of growing ROMA, must also be referred to an early period. But after that, and until the change from a republic to a despotism, the regulations of the coinage were such as to make it impossible now to arrange the coins in chronological order. The operations of the mint were under the control of the Senate, and by that body intrusted to an official board, who seem to have had the power to enstamp such devices as they chose, but not to place the head or effigy of any individual on the coin, as was then the practice in neighboring monarchies. This distinction, it may be observed, has prevailed down to this day; and it is to the precedent set by the republics of Greece and Rome, as well as to an obvious propriety, that we owe the rule which excludes from our coins the heads of the Presidents. But while this honor was denied even to a consul or a conqueror, the Senate permitted, or overlooked, the insertion in the legend of the *name* of an officer of the mint, or of a consul, prætor, or provincial governor, for whose disbursements any specific grant of bullion was wrought into coin; or, if not an individual name, a general family surname; to which was frequently added some device to illustrate a famous action of the man, or of his ancestor. This evasion of the strict republican rule does not, however, give much aid to the numismatist, especially where the name and exploit were those of an ancestor, or where the same name belongs to persons of different eras. The whole difficulty in the case has, by common consent, long since been resolved into a classification of such pieces as FAMILY Coins, in opposition to Imperial; and they are anomalously arranged in the *alphabetical order* of family names. The limit of this arrangement is not exactly defined, but it may be said to extend almost from the commencement of the use of silver down to the days of Augustus; although the rule in regard to portraits was broken through by his predecessor.

The *family coins* may, therefore, represent a period of two hundred and fifty years, terminating about the birth of Christ.

Augustus took charge of the gold and silver coinage as an imperial prerogative, leaving the brass still under the care of the Senate; a most striking exemplification of the change of affairs, and of the relative power of prince and people. This accounts for the S. C. (senatus consulto) on the inferior moneys. After the time of Gallienus, about the middle of the third Christian century, even this remnant of Senatorial authority disappears.

In respect to the date of Roman coins, it is to be noticed, generally, that although the art of coining probably originated in Greece or Asia Minor, about the time of the foundation of the Roman colony, it appears not to have reached that obscure and rude people until the reign of Servius Tullius, near the close of the second century of Rome. Reckoning from that term as far downward as we can verify the coinage of the Lower Empire, which is not nearer to its overthrow than a century and a half, the range of date is more than eighteen hundred years. It may be added, that there is no single series to be compared with it, in extent, variety, and completeness. There was scarcely an emperor, or usurper, though hurled from his seat in a fortnight or a month, who did not leave a diversity of monetary monuments for coming ages.

But more particularly, as to the date of any individual piece, it is ascertained, in many cases, by the year of the "tribunitian power" of the Emperor; thus, TR. P. VI. of Claudius is equivalent to A. D. 46. It is solved also by the year of his consulship; thus, Vespasian Cos. III. answers to A. D. 71: but as that title was not annually resumed like the preceding, this is a less direct means of information. The renewal of the inaugural vow, every five or ten years (VOT. V., VOT. X.), likewise determines the date. And when a victory, or other great event, is symbolized on the coin, its age is determined by the aid of history. But often we can only approach the date within a few years, that is, within the limits of a reign; and the brevity of many of them gives even more precision than an annual mark.

Notwithstanding the large use made of emblems in allusion to Christianity, from and after the time of Constantine, there is no instance of a Christian date on a Roman coin; nor, indeed, is it to be found on the coinage of any country, until a period subsequent to the fall of the Lower Empire.

II. THE MATERIAL, or COMPOSITION, of Roman coins.—For about three centuries, Roman money consisted solely of bronze, a mixture of copper and tin; at first cast in moulds, but afterwards stamped, when other metals came into use. In the year of Rome 487 (B. C. 266) silver was introduced into the coinage, and gold sixty years later; though it is believed that this last was of trifling amount prior to the conquests of Julius Cæsar. In his time, bronze coins began to be displaced by copper and brass; the latter, a composition of copper and calamine (ore of zinc), being wrought with some trouble, and much admired, is said to have been accounted worth twice as much as copper. This mixture disappeared about the close of the third Christian century, and thereafter copper alone was used for the inferior coinage.

The gold coin was maintained at almost absolute purity (990 to 995 thousandths) from first to last. The exceptions in our collection are in the instance of Michael I. Rhangabe (A. D. 811 – 813), who, besides a bezant of good weight and fineness, issued one very inferior in both respects, the fineness being not above 600; and again, in the reigns of Michael VII., Ducas, Romanus IV., and Nicephorus III., extending from 1067 to 1081, we have gold coins of the same inferior quality. They were restored by the next prince, Alexius I.

The silver coin, down to the reign of Augustus inclusive, was also intended and considered as pure, and is found to be 950 to 985 thousandths fine. But in the ensuing reigns there was a constant downward tendency, ending in an absurd and extravagant debasement. In the coinage of Nero, we find the quality of 82 per cent.; from Vespasian to Hadrian, it ranges from 78 to 85. The *very* base silver begins with Septimus Severus, about A. D. 200; and in the times of Elagabalus and Philip (say half a century farther on), the coins contained not more than 40 to 45 per cent. of silver; the alloy being copper, with a portion of tin, to preserve the color. In some cases it would seem as if the emperors of those troubled times resorted to the expedient of issuing copper with a mere plating of silver. But a salutary and permanent reform is to be dated from the reign of Diocletian, in the close of the third century. Silver of a good quality, say 91 to 96 per cent. fine, was used from that time, down through all the decline of the empire.* The silver coin appears, however, not to have been abundant in the later times; the currency chiefly consisting of gold for large payments, and copper for petty dealings. This is fairly inferred from the proportions in which the three kinds are now extant, or are from time to time recovered.

III. Denomination and Value.—As it regards the denominations of Roman coins, the modifications and changes, in a range of eighteen centuries, have occasioned so much perplexity, that the professed collectors pay but little attention to the subject, finding it more convenient to use their own technical terms; such as, *gold* (or *silver*) *of the usual size;* gold or silver *quinarius*, half-size; *large medallions*, *small medallions; first*, *second*, and *third brass;* or *large*, *middle*, and *small brass*. The expressions are not very definite, but sufficiently so for their purposes. So as to intrinsic value; whether a gold piece is 12 to 24 carats, whether a silver one is pure or base, is a circumstance which they hardly deign to inquire into; the degree of rarity is every thing.

But every intelligent reader of the history of Rome wishes to have

---

* The degrees of fineness above stated are from our own trials; by assay, in the case of silver coins not valuable; by specific gravity, where the pieces were too scarce to be cut; a very good approximation for gold coins, and sufficient for rare silver. Whatever difference there is between our rates and those to be found in the Preface of Akerman on Roman Coins (and it is not important) is chargeable to the very unsteady character of the coins, even of the same reign; possibly of the same year. The weights (hereafter given) are also our own, and show about the same correspondence with those given by Akerman.

We have found also, in the silver coins, a larger quantity of gold than would be suffered to remain in the present state of the *parting* art. It is small enough, however, to show that the ancients took some pains in that business.

some idea of the moneys according to their names, which he meets on every page ; as also of their intrinsic value. A few details must suffice here.

As, *sestertius*, *denarius*, *aureus*, were the principal money-terms of the Romans.

The *as*, or *æs libralis*, " pound of brass," and its divisions, were the earliest coins. Originally the *as* weighed a Roman pound of 12 oz. (equal to 12 oz. avoird.), but, by successive reductions in a long course of years, it was brought down to half an ounce, before the Christian era. In this form it was often called by the diminutive term *assarium*. In the time of Constantine it had declined to 20 grains.

The *sestertius*, called also *nummus*, " the coin," by eminence, was a brass coin, of about one ounce in the time of Augustus, and so continued for two centuries, when it began to lose weight, and is not easily to be traced. The Romans were used to reckon by the sestertius for small sums, and by the *sestertium*, or great sesterce (equal to 1,000 sestertii), for large amounts. This last was only a money of account.

The *denarius* was the principal silver coin, weighing at first about 60 grains, and, although rather lighter than the Greek drachm, passed as its equivalent. In the second Christian century it weighed 50 to 55 grains; in the third, 48 to 50. The fineness being also in a course of depreciation, the value of the piece, at first near 16 cents, fell, under the first emperors, to 14 or 15 cents ; 11 or 12 in the times of Vespasian, Trajan, and the Antonines ; and about 6 cents, under Elagabalus. Its character was somewhat restored by Diocletian ; but it seems impossible, from the great fluctuation in weight, to put a value upon the denarius of the Empire after its partition.*

From this coin we ascertain the value of inferior ones already named. It was at first worth ten times the *as;* but afterwards, and before the Christian era, was equal to 16 *asses*. It was also equal to four *sestertii*, or two *quinarii*. The quinarius was a silver coin, not very common.

The *aureus*, or gold coin, was double the weight of the denarius, under the first emperors, and intrinsically worth about five dollars; sometimes a quarter-dollar more, but oftener less by that much. So it continued down to Pertinax, A. D. 192, as we find from our own specimens, and as we learn from other sources, until Severus Alexander, thirty years later. During that century the gold coinage partook somewhat of the confusion, and especially the depreciation, of the other moneys. The aurei in our cabinet, from Decius to Numerian, vary 20 grains (85 cents) one from another, and on the average are worth about $ 3.25. From

---

* It seems to be taken for granted, while it is by no means certain, that the English penny was based upon the later Roman denarius. The early pennies weigh nearly a pennyweight, and are worth six cents. The coin has since passed from silver to copper, and is worth only two cents. And (to trace the lineage down to our own day and country), by the debasement of moneys of account, the *penny* in the United States, though differing in different States, is so little above a cent that it is common to use the two terms interchangeably. We may remark here that the translation of the word *denarion* (denarius) into *penny*, in the New Testament, although in one sense legitimate, gives a very incorrect idea.

Diocletian to Constantine the Great, the aureus, now assuming the name of *solidus*, is about $ 3.50. But it was again reduced, by the sons of Constantine, to 70 grains, or three dollars value; and, singularly enough, maintained that weight, within a grain or two, during eight or nine centuries thereafter. The gold solidus, or *bezant* of the Byzantine Empire, was the currency of all Europe in the Middle Ages, and is often met with in the histories of those eventful times; and (except in one or two cases of gross deterioration of fineness) may be understood as a piece of nearly fine gold, about three dollars in value, or, more exactly, $ 2.90.

IV. THE MEANING OF THE DEVICES naturally attracts attention, and has been so much a study, that, in most cases, in spite of much obscurity and abbreviation, it is pretty well known what was intended to be expressed or symbolized. It might interest, or at least amuse, the unskilful, to see an antiquarian set himself to work upon such an unpromising row of initials as S. P. Q. R. P. P. OB C. S., and alight upon this solution, — *Senatus Populus Que Romanus, Patri Patriæ, Ob Cives Servatos*, meaning, in extenso, that the Senate and people of Rome thanked their emperor, the father of his country, for preserving the citizens; a compliment repeatedly found on the coins of Augustus Cæsar and Caligula.* In respect to the legends, nothing more need here be said, as they are generally copied into the ensuing descriptions, with an occasional translation, for those who are not accustomed to the extreme *density* of a Latin inscription.

Some idea of the devices may be obtained from the few specimens engraved in the frontispiece. The helmeted head of an imaginary deity, or personification of Rome, was the favorite obverse of the republican coinage, as the emperor's portrait was in the imperial days. On the reverse, we are continually reminded that the Romans were a warlike and an idolatrous people; the allusions being almost entirely to their gods or their arms. This is the case as far as to Constantine, under whose authority Christianity was adopted as the state religion; from his time, (excepting in the brief reign of Julian, who made a determined effort to restore Jupiter and Apis,) we see no more of the ancient divinities, although there is an abundance of the usual GLORIA ROMANORUM and VICTORIA AUGUSTI, much more indeed than faithful history warrants. After a time, even military glory seems sunk in the superior claims of piety, and the rude coins of the declining Eastern Empire almost slight the reigning emperor, in a wretched delineation of the form of our Saviour, or of the Virgin, with such mottoes as JESUS CHRISTUS, REX REGNANTIUM.

It may here be added, that the Byzantine coins offer some mysteries which have hitherto baffled the numismatists; especially the colossal

* This abbreviated style has but lately gone out of fashion; that is, since monarchs have contented themselves with fewer titles, and less glorification. Who would suppose that under the letters M. B. F. ET H. REX, F. D. B. ET L. D. S. R. I. A. T. ET E., found on the guineas of George III., there should be couched such a crowd of dignities as — "King of Great Britain, France, and Ireland; Defender of the Faith; Duke of Brunswick and Luneburg; Arch Treasurer and Elector of the Holy Roman Empire"?

letters M and K, on the reverse of the copper, for which there is no satisfactory interpretation.

V. Style of Execution. — The encomiums of amateurs prepare us for a severe disappointment, when we come for the first time to inspect the coins of Rome. Their appearance is much below what would be expected from the reputation of Roman arts and civilization. There is, it is true, a wide diversity of skill exhibited in the die-sinking branch. Many of the heads are admirable, even to a cultivated taste and eye of modern times; and in general, as far down as to Constantine, there is a good deal of character and evident approach to a real portrait, even where the finish is rather barbarous. But the reverse side of the coin was evidently handed over to the apprentices, and, with occasional exceptions, is beneath criticism.

That Rome certainly had artists capable of exquisite engraving, we know from the long and large series of gems still extant. The inquiry, why there should be such a difference between the gems and the coins, is most probably to be solved by such an answer as this, that the *masters* of the art, imported from Greece, were but few in number, and the public taste did not exact much skill for the coinage, the principal office of which was to pass from hand to hand in barter, and not to be kept for show. It has been so almost down to our own day. The guineas and shillings of the last century, the Spanish dollars and fractions of this, are not worthy to stand as specimens of the general state of arts.

From and after the sons of Constantine, the style of execution continually deteriorates; and we are left to wonder that a people not destitute of letters could tolerate such a burlesque of coinage. Though there were but few of the emperors who were so fortunate as to transmit their throne, with their face, to a son or near relation, the portraits present a long gallery of striking similitudes. On taking up a large brass coin of the great Justinian, the oracle of lawyers, we seem to behold the visage and the workmanship of an untutored Indian.

The other and more mechanical parts of the mintage (and this will apply to Greek as well as Roman) allow of no higher praise. Unless coins are so shaped as to lie flat, and admit of being piled one upon another, and render apparent any diminution by filing or clipping, they are not well fitted for their proper uses. These objections apply very generally to ancient coins. Other faults, chargeable to the want of machinery and metallurgic skill, need not be dwelt upon. (Manual of Coins, p. 12.)

VI. The present degree of rarity of Roman coins is worth a passing notice. No one need suppose that there was any scarcity of such coins in their own day, and especially in the flourishing era of the earlier emperors. There was a vast population (Gibbon estimates the population of the Roman Empire at one hundred and twenty millions, in the time of Claudius) and no paper money; and yet the scale of prices was not materially different from what it is in Europe at this day. "A penny a day," that is, a denarius, is as good pay for a laborer in Switzerland, as it was in Judea. Julius Cæsar could, on a single occasion, afford a present or donative to each foot soldier, of about eight hundred dollars;

and to each equestrian four times that sum.* Nero spent some eighty millions of dollars in this way; and when the vacant empire was put up at auction, a bid equal to eight hundred dollars to each pretorian soldier secured it to Didius Julianus.

The activity of the mints, and the variety of dies or devices for the coins, are most astonishing. There is no parallel to it in our own day. Let it suffice to say, that there are now extant, of the Emperor Commodus (A. D. 180 – 192), of such only as are considered rather rare, sixty-eight varieties of gold, sixty of silver, and a still larger number in brass; while of his successor Pertinax, who reigned but three months, there are gold coins of eight different dies, silver of twelve, and brass of seventeen. The whole catalogue of Roman dignitaries, whose coins remain to the present time, embracing emperors or "Augusti," vice-emperors or "Cæsares," empresses, and usurpers, numbers two hundred and seven names; counting from Julius Cæsar down to the subversion of the Eastern and Western divisions of the Empire. Of the consular or family coins there are about twenty-five hundred varieties. Altogetner, from the earliest *as* to the latest *bezant*, there must be at least ten thousand different types.†

It will, therefore, occasion no surprise, that, though so many centuries have elapsed, and nearly every other monument of this wonderful empire has perished, there are coins enough remaining to made up a great many cabinets, public and private, and to form a regular market, and an established branch of trade.‡ The tariff of ancient coins is adjusted to their interest and rarity, and is as well understood and regulated as the prices in any kind of business. Formerly it was sufficient to marshal them under five or six degrees or divisions of scarceness; more modern assiduity and refinement have doubled the number. Thus we have first, V. C., very common; then C., common; then S., scarce; then R. 1, and so on to R. 8, or eighth rarity; which last distinction belongs to an *unique*, and perhaps goes as far as a quadruplicate, or one of four. The highest degree which our collection can boast, if it be worth a boast, is the sixth rarity; but it is in a very few instances.

The present degree of rarity of ancient coins, to speak in a general way, is to be inferred from the market price of the commonest kinds. Silver coins of Augustus and Tiberius, for example, if in good preservation, can be had in Europe for twice or thrice their intrinsic value; say thirty to fifty cents. The drachms of Alexander the Great, though now near twenty-two hundred years old, may be obtained in Constantinople for fifty cents, thrice the value of the silver. The copper coins of Con-

---

* A prodigious outlay, if we consider the size of the army. The peace establishment of Hadrian was thirty legions, supposed to count three hundred and seventy-five thousand men; with a probable naval force of seventy-five thousand more.

† Mionnet, De la Rareté et du Prix des Medailles Romaines, Paris, 1827; also Akerman, an English work on the same subject, 1834.

‡ The banks of deposit possessed by the ancients were such as were likely to be broken only by the ploughshare or the railroad excavations of ages then to come. Roman coins are thus in constant course of discovery, and are found in Britain and Hindostan, as well as through the vast space between.

stantine and his sons are so abundant, that a person may supply himself with them at four or five cents a piece, or less by the quantity, and run no risk of being imposed upon with counterfeits.

But if the fancy of the amateur runs upon the rarer types, he may soon lavish a fortune. And here the writer will hazard the opinion, that there is a great deal of false taste, as well as extravagant outlay, in this particular. To tell the truth, collectors too often prize a coin less on account of its own historical, artistical, or intrinsic value, or all these combined, than on account of its mere rarity. There is a rage to possess a coin which nobody else possesses. Persons to whom this subject is new will be amazed to hear that a silver coin of Maxentius, of rare reverse, brought £ 18, or 87 dollars, at a public sale in London; and that a small gold coin of Allectus, an obscure and transient usurper in Britain (A.D. 293–295), concerning whom history has hardly thought it worth while to record a line, brought £ 74, or 358 dollars (Akerman, under *Maxentius* and *Allectus*); and, to crown all, that, at the famous "Trattle Sale" in 1832, a trial-piece, engraved by Thomas Simon for Charles II., "a very fine specimen," sold for £ 225, or 1,089 dollars. (Jewitt, Hand-book of British Coins.—It was in the same spirit that a copy of Boccaccio's Decameron, printed in 1471, was contended for at a London auction in 1812, by three noble lords; and was knocked off to one of them for £ 2,260, equal to *eleven thousand dollars.*) This may be regarded as suitable sport for nobles of princely fortune, in search of imaginary "gems," but certainly would do no credit to the taste and judgment of sober amateurs.

I have ventured to depart from numismatic usage in one particular, of no great importance. The coins of Greek cities, of a date subsequent to their incorporation into the Roman Empire, and bearing little else than the imperial head and titles, have been withdrawn from the department of Greek republican coins, and placed with the Roman under their respective emperors. Their proper position would be a nice point to argue, if it were worth an argument. But (without summing up the reasons) I apprehend that the democratic taste will justify a distinction between the potin of Antioch and the silver of Athens.

The collection contains a small number of acknowledged counterfeits, nearly all of imperial coins, and all from the manufactory of Mr. Becker, of Berlin. This eminent amateur of coins has conceived and effected the project of supplying collectors with *copies* of such pieces as by their rarity and high price are hardly to be procured; and for this purpose, aided no doubt by the prospect of a lucrative trade, has caused to be engraved the vast number of 510 dies, for the coinage of 255 different specimens, chiefly antique. These are, without doubt, the best efforts at counterfeiting, and the least dishonest; but a little familiarity is sufficient to detect them, as a slight reflection is enough to reprobate them. They came to us as part of a large lot, and are retained, as showing what the originals are, and as affording facilities for acquiring the art of discrimination, a very important part of the collector's work. It is a satisfaction to know that the utmost skill of man is inadequate to the confounding of truth and error, where diligence and experience are set in opposition.* It should be added that these pieces are mostly of the usurpers, and "emperors for a day," and therefore of little historical interest.

The copies or counterfeits by Becker are designated by *cb* in the description.

℞ is an abbreviation for *reverse.*

When the metal is not specified, it is to be understood as the same as that of the coin immediately previous.

Where the reverse has been omitted, it was to avoid repetition or unimportant detail.

DIVISION I.

ERA OF THE REPUBLIC.†

ALL the coins of this era, except the earliest bronze, and the earliest silver, (which last are known by the simple inscription ROMA,) are arranged under family names. As far as known, there are about one hundred and seventy-five families represented in coins still extant, of which one hundred and twenty-six are in this collection. As an example of the mode of arrangement, the pieces which bear the names A. POST. (Aulus Postumius) and C. POST. (Caius Postumius) are placed together, under the title POSTUMIA. If the cognomen only is given, as in the case of BRVTVS, on various types of Marcus Junius Brutus, it is nevertheless referred to the well-known family name, JUNIA. And by the same rule, certain coins of Julius Cæsar are retained in the family JULIA.

The types in this series are not generally of the most common kind, and would repay the inspection of a practised numismatist. For the more general reader, we have occasionally interrupted the roll, to call attention to a specimen of historical interest.

3. TRIENS, or piece of four ounces, indicated by the four dots under the rude figure of a ship. Very early coinage. Bronze. 4, 5. SEXTANS, of two ounces. Bronze. 6. UNCIA, ounce. Small size. Br. 7, 8. TRIENS. Small. Br. 9. SEXTANS, of Campania. Br. 10, 11. ROMA, silver denarii. 12. ROMA, silver quinarius. 13. ABURIA. This and the following specimens in this division are all silver denarii, except where otherwise mentioned. 14. ACCOLEIA. 15, 16. ACILIA. 17. ÆLIA. 18, 19, 20. ÆMILIA. 21. AFRANIA. 22. ALLIA.

---

* A full account of "Die Becker'schen falschen Münz Stämpel" is contained in a pamphlet by Prof. von Steinbüchel, Vienna, 1836. The general price of his silver coin is 1½ florins of Austria, or 73 cents; gold pieces are from 7½ to 12 florins.

† This word is used in opposition to the *imperial* era, and in the modern sense. Even under the most grinding despotism, Rome always flattered herself with the title of "Republic." The coins of Julian celebrate the *Securitas Reipublicæ.*

23, 24. ANNIA. (The latter in brass.) 25. ANTESTIA. 26. ANTIA. 27. ANTONIA. (The legionary coins of Mark Antony, usually placed here, have been transferred to the next division.) 28. APRONIA. Brass. 29, 30. AQUILLIA. ℞ of No. 30 shows a woman kneeling before a soldier; underneath, SICIL. This commemorates the suppression of a noted revolt of the slaves in Sicily, by Manlius Aquillus.

31. ASINIA. Brass. 32. ATTILIA. 33. AURELIA. 34. BŒBIA. 35, 36, 37. CÆCILIA. 38. CÆCINIA. Brass. 39. CÆSIA. 40. CALIDIA. 41. CALPURNIA. ℞. A horseman riding at full speed; an ear of wheat above; legend L. PISO FRUGI. In the year of Rome 507 there was a great scarcity of food in the city, and Calpurnius Piso was despatched to Africa to purchase corn. This trivial honor is magnified by no less than one hundred and thirty varieties of denarii. 42, 43. CARISIA. 44, 45, 46. CASSIA. 47. CESTIA. *cb.* 48. CIPIA. 49, 50, 51. CLAUDIA. 52. CLAUDIA. *cb.* 53. CLOVIA. Brass. 54, 55. CLOULIA. The latter a quinarius. 56. CŒLIA. 57. CONSIDIA. 58. COPONIA. 59, 60, 61. CORDIA.

62-65. CORNELIA. 66. CREPERIA. 67, 68. CREPUSIA. 69. CUPIENA. 70. CURIATIA. 71. CURTIA. 72. DIDIA. 73. DOMITIA. 74, 75. EGNATIA. 76. EGNATULEIA. 77. EPPIA. 78. FABIA. 79. FANNIA. 80. FARSOLEIA. 81. FLAMINIA. 82. FLAVIA. 83, 84. FONTEIA. 85. FUFIA. 86. FULVIA. 87. FUNDANIA. 88, 89, 90. FURIA. 91. GELLIA. 92. HERENNIA. 93. HORATIA. *cb.* 94. HOSIDIA. 95, 96. HOSTILIA. In a battle with the Vientes (in the early days of the republic), the Roman troops were seized with a panic, and in his extremity Tullus Hostilius, their leader, offered his vows to Pallor and Pavor, the gods of *fear* and *trembling*. Two terrified heads display these attributes. On the reverse is the name of L. Hostilius Saserna, a descendant of Tullus, and an officer of Julius Cæsar; for this person they were evidently coined. 97. JULIA. 98-101. JUNIA. No. 98, a remarkable type, is a coin of Marcus Brutus, and commemorates the fact that his ancestor, L. Junius Brutus, was the first Consul of Rome. He is seen guarded by lictors, and preceded by a herald. 102-105. LICINIA. 106. LIVINEIA. 107. LUCILIA. 108, 109. LUCRETIA. 110. LURIA. Brass. 111. LUTATIA. 112. MÆCILIA. Brass. 113. MÆNIA. 114. MAIANIA. 115. MAMILIA. 116. MANLIA. 117-119. MARCIA. 120. MARIA. 121, 122. MEMMIA. 123, 124. MINUTIA. 125. MUSSIDIA. 126. NÆVIA. 127. NONIA. 128. NORBANUS. 129. NORBANUS. *cb.* 130. NUMONIA. *cb.* 131. OPEIMIA. 132-134. PAPIA. 135. PAPIRIA. 136. PEDANIA. 137, 138. PETILLIA. 139. PETRONIA. 140. PINARIA. 141. PLÆTORIA. 142. PLANCIA. 143-145. PLAUTIA. 146. POBLICIA. 147, 148. POMPEIA. 149, 150. POMPONIA. 151, 152. PORCIA. The Porcian law, declared in the year of Rome 453, exempted Roman citizens from the indignity of scourging. ℞ of No. 152 represents a citizen protected by a magistrate from the lictor, and underneath, the word PROVOCO, "I appeal." (See in the New Testament, Acts xxii. 24-27, where the Apostle Paul availed himself of this immunity.) 153-155. POS-

TUMIA. 156, 157. PROCILIA. 158, 159. QUINCTIA. 160. RENIA. 161. ROSCIA. 162. RUBRIA. 163, 164. RUSTIA. 165. RUTILIA. 166. SATRIENUS. 167. SCRIBONIA. 168. SEMPRONIA. 169. SENTIA. 170. SERGIA. 171 - 173. SERVILIA. 174. SICINIA. 175. SILIA. 176. SPURILIA. 177. SULPICIA. 178. TERENTIA. 179. THORIA. 180. TITIA. 181, 182. TITURIA. ℞ of the first represents two soldiers throwing their shields upon a prostrate female. The city of Rome was betrayed to the Sabines by Tarpeia, on condition of receiving "what they wore on their left arms," intending their gold bracelets. As soon as the city was taken, the soldiers, to fulfil their vow and punish her perfidy, threw upon her their bracelets *and shields*, and she was crushed to death. The place was afterwards famous as the "Tarpeian Rock." ℞ of the second represents the Romans carrying off the Sabine women. The family Tituria traced their descent from the Sabines. 183. TREBANIA. 184. TALLIA. 185 - 188. VALERIA. (The last is brass.) 189. VARGUNTEIA. 190. VETTIA. 191. VETTURIA. 192 - 194. VIBIA. 195. VIBIA. *cb.* 196 - 198. VOLTEIA. 199 - 202. Uncertain. Two are of base metal.

DIVISION II.

JULIUS CÆSAR TO TRAJAN (INCLUSIVE). B. C. 49 TO A. D. 117.

I. CAIUS JULIUS CÆSAR was born in the year of Rome 654 (B. C. 100). Created Triumvir, with Pompey and Crassus, at the age of forty, and Dictator at fifty-two. He was made Perpetual Dictator B. C. 44, and assassinated in the same year, aged fifty-six.

1. Gold. Head of Julius. DICT(ator) PERP(etuo). PON(tifex) MAX(imus). ℞. Head of Caius (Octavius). 2. Silver. Æneas carrying Anchises. 3. Dictator the second time. 4. Head of Julius veiled. Perp. Dictator. 5. Julius crowned. Perp. Dictator. 6. Pontifical Instruments. ℞. Elephant. 7. Brass. JULIUS DIVOS. 8. Silver, of Marcus Brutus the conspirator. Head of the elder Brutus. 9. Brass, of Pompey the Great. ℞. PIUS IMP(erator). Prow of a vessel.

II. Caius Octavius, afterwards AUGUSTUS, grand-nephew of Julius Cæsar, was born B. C. 63. He was joined with Mark Antony and Lepidus in the government, at the death of Julius; became sole master of the Empire, B. C. 31; received the title of Emperor two years after; and died A. D. 14, aged seventy-six.

11. Gold. AUGUSTUS DIVI F. IMP. X. ℞. ACT(ium). Commemorates that decisive battle. 12. Gold, of Sextus Pompey, naval commander, reduced by Augustus, B. C. 36. MAG(nus) PIUS IMP(erator) ITER(um). ℞., heads of Pompey the Great and Cneius. PRÆF(ectus) CLAS(sis) ET ORÆ MARIT(imæ), "Commander of the fleet and sea-coast." Ex S. C. *cb.* 13. Silver; same as the preceding. *cb.* 14. Silver of the same, different type. *cb.* 15. Mark Antony; Cæsar on the reverse. 16. Antony; legends on both sides made up of his titles. 17. Lepidus; Cæsar on the reverse. 18. Augustus. DIVUS JULIUS. 19. The same. ℞. SIGNIS RECEPTIS. 20. Aqueduct on the reverse.

21. ℞. Horses on a triumphal arch. IMP. CÆSAR. 22. ℞. Pontifical instruments. COS. ITER. "Consul a second time." 23. S. P. Q. R. OB CIVES SERVATOS. 24. Fine head of Augustus, without legend. ℞. DIVI F(ilius), "the son of God," probably in reference to the deified Julius. 25. ℞. Horseman at full speed. AUGUST. 26. A Bull. IMP. X., i. e. the title of Imperator, Emperor, conferred the tenth time. It was then merely a military distinction. 27. A quinarius. ℞. ASIA RECEPTA. 28. Brass. ℞. Within a wreath, AUGUSTUS TRIBUNIC(ia) POTEST(ate). 29. DIVUS AUGUSTUS PATER. The deceased Augustus sainted, or deified. ℞. S. C. (Senatus Consulto.) 30. Silver, of Agrippa, son-in-law of Augustus. *cb.* 31. Brass, of Agrippa. Consul third time. 32. Silver. Caius and Lucius, grandsons of Augustus. 35 – 54. Twenty silver coins of Mark Antony, the series struck for the respective legions under his command. The reverse shows a ship, or military ensigns, with the number of the legion, as LEG. VI., &c. They were probably used in payment of the troops, and otherwise served to display the power of the general. Four of the series are wanting.

III. TIBERIUS CÆSAR, son of the Empress Livia, was adopted by Augustus, A. D. 4, and succeeded to the Empire A. D. 14, at the age of fifty-six. While on a sick-bed, he was smothered at the instigation of Caligula, which finished a cruel reign of nearly twenty-three years. (A. D. 37.)

55. Gold. TI. CÆSAR DIVI. AUG. F(ilius) AUGUSTUS. ℞. PONTIFEX MAXIMUS. 56. The same type in silver. 57. Base silver or *potin* struck at Alexandria in Egypt; legends in Greek. 58. Large brass. An altar, with figures of Victory. 59, 60. Brass, with the usual legends, and ℞. S. C. 61. Silver, of Drusus, son of the Emperor. (Poisoned by his wife, A. D. 23.) ℞. Head of Tiberius. *cb.* 62. Brass, of Drusus. ℞. S. C. 63. Livia, mother of Tiberius. SALUS AUGUSTA. (Died A. D. 29, aged eighty-six.) 64. Silver. Antonia, daughter of Mark Antony, and mother of the Emperor Claudius. ANTONIA AUGUSTA. (Poisoned, A. D. 38, aged seventy-six.) *cb.* 65. Brass, of the same. 66. Silver. Germanicus, son of Antonia, and nephew of Tiberius, who adopted him. (Poisoned, A. D. 19, by the governor of Syria.) *cb.* 67, 68. Brass, of the same. 69. Large brass. Agrippina, sen., wife of Germanicus, and granddaughter of Augustus. (Exiled, and starved to death by Tiberius, A. D. 33, aged forty-eight.) 70. Brass. NERO ET DRUSUS, CÆSARES. Sons of Germanicus, and brothers of Caligula. (Nero died in exile, A. D. 30; Drusus was starved by order of Tiberius, A. D. 33.)

IV. Caius Cæsar, called CALIGULA (from his military dress), was adopted by his grand-uncle Tiberius; whom he succeeded, A. D. 37, at the age of twenty-five. His oppressive reign was cut short by an assassin, A. D. 41.

72. Silver. C. CÆSAR AUG. ℞. S. P. Q. R. P. P. OB C. S., i. e. "the Senate and People of Rome, to the Father of his Country, for preserving the citizens." 73. Brass. Usual legend. ℞. Vesta, seated.

V. Tiberius CLAUDIUS, nephew of Tiberius, was born at Lyons, B. C. 10, and succeeded to the Empire A. D. 41. He married his niece, Agrippina the younger, A. D. 49, by whom he was poisoned, A. D. 54.

79. Gold. TI. CLAUD. CÆSAR. AUG. P. M. TR. P. VIIII. IMP. VI. ℞. S. P. Q., &c. 80. Silver. Same legend; with GERM(anicus). *cb.* 81. Brass. ℞. LIBERTAS AUGUSTA. 82. Silver. Agrippina, wife of the

Emperor, and mother of Nero. AGRIPPINÆ AUGUSTÆ. Head of Claudius on the reverse. (She was killed by order of Nero, A. D. 59, aged forty-three.) **83.** Agrippina and Nero, face to face. *cb.*

VI. NERO, stepson of Claudius, was declared *Cæsar*, A. D. 50, at the age of thirteen years, and succeeded to the Empire at seventeen. Having become odious through his excesses, and hearing that a successor was elected, he slew himself, A. D. 68.

87. Gold. NERO CÆSAR AUGUSTUS. ℞. JUPPITER (so spelt) CUSTOS, — "Jupiter the Keeper." 88. Silver. NERO CÆSAR. Youthful profile. 90. Large brass. NERO CLAUD. CÆSAR, &c. ROMA on the reverse. Supposed to have been struck on the rebuilding of Rome, after the fire. 91. The temple of Janus closed. PACE P(opulo) R(omano) TERRA MARIque PARTA JANUM CLUSIT. 92. Coined at Alexandria, in Egypt. Greek. 93. Coined at Alexandria, in Cilicia. Greek.

VII. GALBA, born B. C. 3, was governor of Spain under Nero; created Emperor by the army and Senate, A. D. 68; murdered by the guards, after a reign of seven months, A. D. 69.

95. Gold. IMP. SERV(ius) GALBA AUG. ℞. S. P. Q. R., &c. 96. Silver. ℞. LIBERTAS PUBLICA. 97. Brass. Same reverse. 98. Silver. CLODIUS MACER. PROPRÆ(tor) AFRICÆ. This provincial governor declared independence upon the death of Nero, but was reduced and put to death by order of Galba. *cb.*

VIII. OTHO, governor of Lusitania (now Portugal), took part in the revolt against Nero. After following in the train of Galba for a short time, he procured his death, and was proclaimed as his successor. But the Empire had to be disputed with Vitellius; and having suffered a defeat, Otho killed himself, A. D. 69, after a reign of only three months, and in his thirty-seventh year.

103. Silver. IMP(erator) OTHO CÆSAR AUG(ustus) TR(ibun.) P(otestate). ℞. SECURITAS P(opuli) R(omani). By the looks of the head, the artist seems to have aimed to confirm the historical fact that the Emperor wore a wig. 104. ℞. PONT(ifex) MAX(imus). "Sovereign pontiff." 105. ℞. VICTORIA OTHONIS. Otho was thrice victorious before his overthrow at Brixellum. No brass coins of this Emperor have come to light.

IX. VITELLIUS, proclaimed Emperor by the legions in Germany, was successful against Otho, and acknowledged by the Senate, A. D. 69. After eight months of gluttony, he fell by the hands of the soldiers, aged fifty-six.

111. Gold. A(ulus) VITELLIUS GERM(anicus), IMP(erator), AUG(ustus), TR(ib.) P(ot.) ℞. A tripod, with a globe and dolphin on the top, and an eagle beneath; XV VIR SACRIS FACIENDIS. Commemorates his offering sacrifice to the shade of Nero, his patron. 112. Silver. Same as the preceding. 113. ℞. FIDES EXERCITUM. Two hands joined, in token of the *faith of the army.* 114. Heads of the two children of Vitellius. LIBERI IMP., &c. *cb.*

X. VESPASIAN was created governor of Judea by Nero, A. D. 66, and became Emperor on the death of Vitellius; died A. D. 79, in his seventieth year, having reigned ten years.

119. Gold. IMP. CÆSAR VESPASIANUS AUG. ℞. CONS(ul) ITER(um) TR(ib.) POT(estate). 120. Silver. ℞. Pontifical Instruments. AUGUR. PONT. MAX. 121. JOVIS CUSTOS. 122. VICTORIA AUGUSTI. 123. A *congius* (a dry measure of about a half-peck) with ears of wheat standing out of it. Expresses his distribution of congiaries, or gifts of corn, to the Roman populace. 124. A veiled female beside a palm-tree.

JUDÆA DEVICTA. Commemorates the destruction of Jerusalem, A. D. 70, by Titus. 125. Consul the seventh time. 126. Figure of Capricorn, under which sign Vespasian was born. DIVUS AUGUSTUS VESPASIANUS. Apotheosis of the deceased Emperor. 127. DIVA DOMITILLA AUGUSTA. Domitilla was married to Vespasian, A. D. 40, and died before his accession. She was afterwards deified. *cb.*

XI. TITUS succeeded his father, A. D. 79, at twenty-eight years. A change of character made him a good prince; but the Romans enjoyed the benefit of it only two years. His death was not without suspicion of poisoning, by Domitian.

135. Gold. T. CÆSAR IMP. VESPASIAN. ℞. COS. IIII. (Fourth year of his consulate.) 136. Silver. CERES AUGUST. 137. A soldier standing on the head of a captive. 138. A statue on a pillar; usual legends. 139. Capricorn. 140. Curule chair. 141. Brass. ÆQUITAS AUGUSTI. 142. Brass. CERES AUGUST. 143. Silver. Julia, daughter of Titus, and after his death a concubine of her uncle Domitian. On the ℞. is a peacock, the emblem of female deification; which honor was conferred on her by Domitian. *cb.* 144. Brass, of Julia.

XII. DOMITIAN, brother of Titus, succeeded to the Empire at the age of thirty, A. D. 81, and reigned fifteen years. He fell by a conspiracy of his household; and though universally detested, received the usual honor of deification. He was the last of "the twelve Cæsars," a classification more popular than proper.

151. Gold. CÆS. AUG. DOMIT. COS. III. ℞. PRINCEPS JUVENTUTIS. The title "Prince of Youth" was given by his father, A. D. 69. 152. Silver. ℞. A dolphin and anchor; usual titles. 153. Copy of an equestrian statue. 154. Victory holding a buckler. 155. COS. XIIII. LUD(os) SÆC(ulares) FEC(it). Alludes to his celebration of the secular games. 156. Brass. The same subject. Priest and musicians. 157. Silver. Domitia, wife of the Emperor.

XIII. NERVA was called to the Empire by the Senate, in his sixty-fourth year, A. D. 96. His virtuous but feeble administration was strengthened by the association of Trajan. After a reign of two years only, he was allowed the distinction of dying a natural death, and was voted a deity. A. D. 98.

159. Gold. IMP. NERVA CÆS. AUG. P(ontifex) M(ax.) TR(ib.) POT(estate). ℞. Pontifical instruments. COS. III. PATER PATRIÆ. 160. Silver. The same type. 161. ÆQUITAS AUGUST(i). 162. FORTUNA AUGUST(i). 163. Two hands joined. CONCORDIA EXERCITUUM. Expresses the ratification by the army of his election; now more important than the voice of the Senate. 164. Brass. The same type.

XIV. TRAJAN, born in Spain, A. D. 53, succeeded Nerva, A. D. 98, and reigned nineteen and a half years. His military exploits, his energy, and leniency (except toward the Christians) endeared him to the Romans as the best of all their emperors, and they early conferred on him the title of OPTIMUS PRINCEPS, which appears on most of his coins. Died in Cilicia, A. D. 117.

167. Gold. IMP. TRAIANO OPTIMO AUG. GER(manicus), DAC(icus), P(ont.) M(ax.) TR. P(otest.) ℞. COS. VI. P(ater) P(atriæ) S. P. Q. R. Germany and Dacia were among his conquests. 168. Silver. Three military ensigns. "The Senate and people of Rome, to the best prince." 169. ℞. Ceres, with legend as above. 170. Equestrian statue. 171. Victory, writing on a shield. 172. PARTHICO, P. M., &c. Expresses his victories in Persia. 173. Front of the Forum, a superb building erected by Trajan. *cb.* 174. The Emperor on a throne, with attendants, assigning kingdoms to three persons below and before him. REGNA

ADSIGNATA. *cb.* 175. PARTHICO DIVI TRAIAN, &c. 176. Victory. (A quinarius.) 177. Large brass. A crowd of titles in the legends. 178. Gold. Plotina, wife of Trajan. (Died A. D. 129, and was one of the few empresses *sans reproche.*) ℞. Vesta seated. *cb.* 179. Silver. Marciana, sister of Trajan. ℞. CONSECRATIO. *cb.* 180. Gold. Matidia, daughter of Marciana, and mother-in-law of the Emperor Hadrian. Plotina on the *rev. cb.* 181. Brass. Greek coin of Trajan and Plotina (Perinthus in Thrace).

DIVISION III.

HADRIAN TO ELAGABALUS. A. D. 117-222.

XV. HADRIAN, through the management of the Empress Plotina, succeeded upon the death of Trajan, A. D. 117. He is noted as the travelling emperor; his long and prosperous reign being spent in marches and journeys to all parts of the Empire. His coins, which are numerous, afford a medallic history of his life. Died in his seventy-second year, and twenty-second of his reign, A. D. 138.

1. Gold. HADRIANUS AUG. Cos. III. Pater Patriæ. ℞. LIBERALITAS AUG(usti). The Emperor was liberal in largesses to the people. 2. Silver. ℞. AFRICA. A female figure, representing Africa, recumbent, Commemorates his visit there. 3. HISPANIA. Figure of Spain, recumbent. 4. RESTITUTORI HISPANIÆ. The Emperor raising a female (Spain) from the ground. 5. ÆGYPTOS. Emblems of Egypt.

6. NILUS. The god of the Nile, recumbent. 7. RESTITUTORI GALLIÆ. The Emperor raising prostrate Gaul. 8. Ceres. 9. Cos. III. Moon and star. 10. The Emperor marching before three soldiers. DISCIPLINA AUG(usti). The army in Germany becoming relaxed in discipline, the Emperor visited them, and inured them to hardships by his own example. *cb.* 11. Brass. ℞. HILARITAS P(opuli) R(omani). A female, holding a stalk of wheat; citizens at her feet. The "hilarity" of the ancient lazzaroni depended very much on the supplies of corn, drawn from the industrious provinces. 12. SALUS AUGUSTA. A female making offerings to a serpent, in behalf of the Emperor's health.

13. Silver, of Sabina, wife of Hadrian. ℞. VENERI GENETRICI. 14. SABINA AUGUSTA, HADRIANI AUG. ℞. CONCORDIA AUG. Commemorates the making up of a quarrel between the Emperor and his wife. They lived so unhappily that she destroyed herself, after a union of thirty-seven years. A. D. 137. 15. Silver, of Ælius Cæsar. He was adopted as Hadrian's successor, but died before him, A. D. 138. 16. Base silver. HAΔPIANOC CEB. Hadrianus Augustus. Coined at Cesarea in Cappadocia.

XVI. ANTONINUS PIUS succeeded Hadrian, by whom he had been adopted, A. D. 138, and reigned twenty-three years. In contrast to the policy of his predecessor, he never travelled farther from Rome than to his villa; but the vast empire was governed with unexampled wisdom and mildness, and it was an age of peace and plenty. His devotion to the gods, and to the memory of his patron, early procured him the surname of PIUS; which became a standing title to all succeeding emperors. The *Christian* religion was openly tolerated. He died A. D. 161, in his seventy-fifth year, universally lamented.

22. Gold. ANTONINUS AUG. PIUS. P. P. ℞. TR. POT. COS. II.

23. Silver. ℞. Italia. A woman sitting on a globe. 24. ℞. The youthful head of Aurelius, who was adopted at the age of seventeen, A. D. 138. 25. ℞. Aurelius more advanced. 26. ℞. A female at an altar. Pietas. 27. Divus Antoninus. ℞. Consecratio. 28. ℞. A funeral pile. Consecratio. 29. ℞. An altar. Divo Pio. The honor of dei fication was eagerly conferred by the Senate. 30. Large brass. ℞. Same as No. 12. 31. Brass. ℞. Romulus and Remus sucking the wolf. 32. Gold. Diva Faustina. Deification of the elder Faustina, wife of Antoninus; born A. D. 105, died 141. 33. Silver. Faustina veiled; Diva Faustina. ℞. Aeternitas. 34. ℞. Junoni Reginæ.

35. ℞. Augusta. 36. Diva Faustina Pia. ℞. A peacock; Consecratio. 37. Brass. ℞. Consecratio. These and other types show the honors paid by the good Emperor to her memory, though while living she occasioned him no little grief and scandal. 38. Brass. Greek coin of Antoninus; Laodicea.

XVII. MARCUS AURELIUS Antoninus, and LUCIUS VERUS, brothers-in-law, who had been of the rank of *Cæsars* for twenty-three years, succeeded A. D. 161, as *Augusti*, colleague Emperors. Though the former was a Stoic philosopher, and the latter a debauchee, they lived without discord, and (as their coins show) were much engaged with the barbarians. The immense Empire was now beginning to tremble with its own weight. Verus died 169, in his fortieth year. Marcus ruled alone for eleven years more, and died at the age of fifty-nine. He was greatly esteemed for his virtues; and "the age of the Antonines" is justly esteemed as a bright one in Roman history.

43. Gold. Aurelius Cæsar Aug. Pii. F. ℞. Tr. Pot. III. Cos. II. 44. Silver. The same legends. 45. Antoninus Aug. Armeniacus. ℞. A female on the ground, personifying captive Armenia. 46. ℞. Victory holding a shield, with the motto Vic. Par. Records the success of the Romans in Parthia. 47. Brass. ℞. A trophy, and two captives seated; De Sarm. The victory over the Sarmatians. 48. Profectio Aug. Emperor on horseback. 49. Silver. Faustina Augusta. ℞. A female with an infant in her arms, and two other children at her feet; Fecund(itas) Augustæ. She was the daughter of Antoninus Pius, and wife of Marcus; died A. D. 175. Her dissolute life could not exempt her from deification. 50. ℞. Sæculi Felicit(as). "The happiness of the age." 51. A fine head of this handsome woman. ℞. Concordia.

52. Brass. ℞. Lætitia. 53. Silver. L. Verus Aug. Armeniacus. ℞. Sundry usual titles. 54. L. Verus Arm. Parth. Max. (The two Emperors were somewhat disposed to conquer per alium, and triumph in persona.) 55. Divus Verus. ℞. Consecratio. 56. Silver, of Lucilla, daughter of Marcus, and wife of Verus. ℞. Vota Publica. 57. ℞. Diana Lucifera.

XVIII. COMMODUS, son of Marcus Aurelius, was admitted to the rank of Cæsar, at five years of age, and of Augustus at sixteen; and succeeded to the Empire in 180, at nineteen years. He gloried chiefly in fighting as a gladiator in the public games, and assumed the name of Hercules. An end was put to his cruelties by assassination, A. D. 192.

64. Gold. M. Commodus Anton(inus) Aug. Pius. ℞. The customary titles. 65. Silver. ℞. Hilaritas. 66. The usual titles. 67. L. Æl(ius) Aurel(ius) Comm(odus). ℞. The club of Hercules; Herculo Romano Augu(sto). 68. Brass. ℞. Sacrificial instruments; Pietas Aug. Records the piety of Commodus. 69. Gold. Crispina Augusta. ℞. Venus Felix. This Empress was banished for gross misconduct,

and afterwards put to death, 183; and was even refused an apotheosis. *cb.* 80. ℞. An altar; DIS GENITALIBUS.

XIX. PERTINAX, the son of a wood-chopper, rose to the highest posts in the army and state, and was declared Emperor upon the death of Commodus, A. D. 192. His virtues were conspicuous; but the iron age of Rome had commenced, and a good ruler could scarcely keep his place. He was murdered by a few soldiers, after a reign of three months, and in his sixty-sixth year.

78. Gold. IMP. CÆS. P. HELV(ius) PERTIN(ax) AUG. ℞. PROVID(entia) DEOR(um). COS. II. 79. Same legends as the gold. *cb.* 80. Brass. Same legends.

XX. DIDIUS JULIANUS, a wealthy citizen of Rome, hearing that the army had offered the Empire at public sale, ran to the camp and outbid a competitor. He was acknowledged by the Senate; and, on the approach of Severus, was deposed and beheaded by the same authority, after a reign of two months, and at sixty years of age, A. D. 193.

85. Gold. IMP. CÆS. M. DID. JULIAN. AUG. ℞. P. M. TR. P. COS. 86. Silver. ℞. RECTOR ORBIS. The Emperor holding a globe. *cb.*
87. Manlia Scantilla, Empress. ℞. JUNO REGINA. "Juno, the Queen." 88, 89. Didia Clara, daughter of Julian. ℞. HILAR(itas) TEMP(orum). The "hilarity of the times" was precarious and intermittent. (89, *cb.*) 90. The same type in brass.

XXI. SEPTIMIUS SEVERUS, a native of Africa, and commander in Germany, was proclaimed Emperor by his legions, on hearing of the death of Pertinax; and, marching to Rome, received the homage of the Senate. He was successful against two powerful competitors, and reigned eighteen years, dying at York, in Britain, A. D. 211, at the age of sixty-five. His surname expressed his character, — severe, and caring little for the opinion of others; yet, on the whole, such a ruler as the times required.

93. Silver. SEVERUS PIUS AUG. ℞. A female seated on a lion; INDULGENTIA AUG(usti) IN CARTH(aginem). The occasion was his investing Carthage with peculiar privileges. 94. ℞. RESTITUTOR URBIS "Restorer of the city." Severus built temples, and restored the secular games in Rome. 95. ℞. Trophy and captives. Legend imperfect.
96. Brass. Usual titles in the legend. 97. Silver, of Julia Domna, wife of Severus. ℞. VENUS GENETRIX. 98. ℞. MATER DEUM. 99. ℞. JUNO. 100. VESTA. 101. Brass, of Julia. MATER DEUM. 102. Greek coin (brass), of Severus; Corcyra, now Corfu. 103. The same; coined at Cesarea, in Cappadocia.

PESCENNIUS NIGER, and CLODIUS ALBINUS, the former governor in Syria, the latter in Britain, started with Severus in the race for the Empire, with powerful armies to back them. Niger was subdued in one year, and Clodius in four, after an obstinate conflict.

104. Gold. IMP. CÆS. C. PESC(ennius) NIGER JUSTUS AUG. ℞. CONCORDIA, P. P. *cb.* (The original of this was unique, and was stolen from the cabinet of the King of France, with other pieces; and has no doubt been melted down. It is proper to add, that, on account of the P. P., to which Niger was not entitled, the original itself was suspected.)
105. Silver. ℞. FORTUNA REDUCI. 106. Moon and stars. SÆCULI FELICIT(as). *cb.* 107. Greek coin of Niger. *cb.* 108. Same, in brass. *cb.* 109. Silver. D. CLOD. SEPT. ALBIN(us) CÆS. 110. ℞. MINER(va) PACIF(era). COS. II. 111. Brass, of Clodius. ℞. Illegible.

XXII. CARACALLA and GETA, sons of Severus, succeeded as joint Emperors, A. D. 211. Their mutual hatred ceased only upon the murder of Gera, in the next year; and Caracalla acted the tyrant alone, for five years longer. He died by the hand of one of his soldiers, at the instigation of Macrinus, while on the march into Persia, A. D. 217, aged thirty years. (*Caracalla*, being a nickname only, never appears on the coins; the true name of this Emperor was Marcus Aurelius Antoninus.)

113. Silver. Imp. Antoninus Aug. ℞. Jovi Conservatori. "To Jupiter the Preserver." 114. Antoninus Pius Aug. Brit(annicus). ℞. Profectio Aug(usti). Caracalla was with the army in North Britain; and figures in Ossian, as "Caracul." 115. Antoninus Pius Aug. Germ(anicus). A quiet retreat through Germany brought him this victorious surname. 116. ℞. Lætitia Publ(ica). "The public joy."

117. ℞. Victor(ia) Antonini Aug. (These four are large denarii, which began to be coined in this reign.) 118. Brass. Usual titles, in the legend. 119. Silver. Plautilla Augusta. (Plautilla was married to Caracalla, A. D. 202; afterwards exiled, and put to death A. D. 212.)

120. ℞. Venus Victrix. 121. ℞. The Emperor and Empress joining hands; Propago Imperi. 122. Brass, of Plautilla. Pietas Aug.

123. Silver. Geta Cæs(ar) Pont. Cos. ℞. Vota Publica. ℞. Princ(eps) Juventutis. (These two were coined before Geta became Emperor.) 124. Sept. Geta Pius Aug. Brit(annicus). ℞. Usual titles. 125. Brass, of Geta. Pontif. Cos. II. 126. Greek coin (brass), of Caracalla, struck at Byzantium.

XXIII. MACRINUS having, for his own safety, procured the murder of Caracalla, was deliberately elected Emperor by the army in Syria, A. D. 217. He was killed the next year, after suffering a defeat by Elagabalus.

127. Silver. Imp. C(æsar) M(arcus) Opel(ius) Sev(erus) Macrinus Aug. ℞. Fides Militum. "Faith of the soldiers." 128. Æquitas Aug(usti). "Equity of the Emperor." 129. Brass. ℞. The Emperor in a quadriga, or car with four horses. 130. Silver, of Diadumenianus, son of Macrinus; created Cæsar and afterwards Augustus, at nine years; shared the fate of his father. *cb.* 131. Brass. ℞. Princ. Juventutis.

XXIV. ELAGABALUS, or Heliogabalus, a boy-priest in the Temple of the Sun, in Syria, and of distant relation to Caracalla, was commended by his mother to the Roman soldiery there, as a son of that Emperor, and by them proclaimed, in opposition to Macrinus. His faction having succeeded, the youth was acknowledged by the Senate, and reigned about four years. He was killed A. D. 222, at the age of about eighteen years, after a course of debauchery and cruelty that is scarcely credible. His real name was Avitus Bassianus, and his imperial name Marcus Antoninus; but he is only known by the designation above, which was the Syrian title of the Sun, as the deity.

135. Silver. Imp. Antoninus Pius Aug. ℞. The Emperor sacrificing; Invictus Sacerdos Aug. "The unconquered priest, Emperor." 136. ℞. The Emperor on horseback. Prof(ectio). Probably his "march" to Rome. 137. ℞. Sacerdos Solis Elagab(ali) dei. He gloried in this character, and introduced the worship of the Sun at Rome.

138. Large silver. ℞. Salus Antonini Aug. 139. Brass. The Emperor in a car. Consul IIII. 141. Large silver. Julia Mæsa Aug. The grandmother of Elagabalus, and by him created a member of the Senate. ℞. Pietas Aug. 142. Silver, of Julia Mæsa. ℞. Pudicitia.

143. The same. ℞. Fecunditas. 144. Julia Soæmias Aug. ℞. Venus Celestis. Julia Soæmias was the mother of the Emperor, and was killed at the same time with him. 145. Julia Paula Aug. ℞. The Emperor and Empress joining hands. Concordia. She was the first wife of Elagabalus, and repudiated in about a year, notwithstanding this "concord." 146. Paula, with Elagabalus on the reverse. *cb.*

147. Julia Aquilia Severa. ℞. Concordia. A vestal virgin, taken by Elagabalus as his second wife; repudiated to make room for a third,

but afterwards recalled. 148. Greek coin, brass, of Elagabalus; struck at Marcianopolis, in Mæsia. 149. Same; struck at Nice, in Bithynia.

DIVISION IV.

SEVERUS ALEXANDER TO CLAUDIUS GOTHICUS. A.D. 222-270.

XXV. SEVERUS ALEXANDER, the cousin of Elagabalus, and adopted by him, succeeded A. D. 222, at the age of seventeen, and reigned thirteen years. The downward course of things was somewhat retarded by this wise and virtuous administration; but was renewed by the barbarous murder of the Emperor, and the elevation of the chief conspirator.

1. Silver. IMP. ALEXANDER PIUS AUG. ℞. SPES PUBLICA. 2. ℞. MARS ULTOR. "Mars, the Revenger." 3. IMP. C. M. AUR. SEV. ALEXAND. AUG. ℞. Usual titles. 4. Brass. ℞. The Emperor in a car. Usual titles. 5. Silver. SALL(ustia) BARBIA ORBIANA AUG. The Emperor on the *rev.* She was the wife of Alexander. *cb.*

6. ℞. CONCORDIA AUGG. 7. Brass, of the same. CONCORDIA AUGUSTORUM. 8. Silver. JULIA MAMÆA. AUG. ℞. FELICITAS PUBLICA. She was the Emperor's mother, and influential in the government. Killed with him. 9. ℞. VENUS VICTRIX. 10. ℞. A female holding an infant. VENERI FELICI. 11. ℞. VESTA. 12. Brass. FELICITAS PUBLICA. 13. Brass, Greek, of Alexander. Byzantium.

XXVI. MAXIMIN I., the Thracian giant, succeeded the prince whose murder he had procured. His successes against the Germans could not atone for his cruel temper, and the Romans declared for GORDIAN and his son, who had assumed the purple in Africa. They were quickly subdued by the forces of Maximin: but, in marching for Rome to encounter a new pair of Emperors, he was murdered by his own soldiers, A. D. 238. He had reigned three years, and was aged sixty-five.

15. Silver. IMP. MAXIMINUS PIUS AUG. ℞. PAX AUGUSTI. 16. ℞. VICTORIA GERM(anica). 17. ℞. FIDES MILITUM. Perhaps alludes to his rescue by the soldiers, when he was sticking fast in a marsh, in Germany. 18. Brass. ℞. SALUS AUGUSTI. 19. ℞. Military standards.

20. Same ℞. as No. 17. 21. Silver. DIVA PAULINA. ℞. A peacock carrying the deceased Empress to heaven. CONSECRATIO. There was some ground for this compliment. 22. JUL(ius) VERUS MAXIMUS CÆS(ar). ℞. PIETAS AUG. This prince was of an opposite disposition to his father, but shared his fate, A.D. 238. 23. Brass, of the same. ℞. PRINCIPI JUVENTUTIS.

XXVII. BALBINUS, a senator, and PUPIENUS, a soldier, both advanced in years, were chosen in Rome to succeed the two Gordians, while Maximin was still living. His defeat confirmed them in the Empire, which they governed wisely; but a mutiny of the soldiers brought them to a violent end, after reigning only about a year, A. D. 239.

29. Large silver. IMP. CÆS. D(ecimus) CÆL(ius) BALBINUS AUG. ℞. Two hands joined; PIÆTAS MUTUA AUGG. "The devotion of the Emperors to each other." 30. ℞. PROVIDENTIA DEORUM. *cb.*

31. IMP. CÆS. M(arcus) CLOD(ius) PUPIENUS AUG. ℞. Two hands joined; PATRES SENATUS (which may mean the Emperors, as "fathers of the Senate," or the Senate, as "the conscript fathers").

32. Small silver of Pupienus. VICTORIA AUGG. *cb.* 33. Brass, of Pupienus. Legend imperfect.

XXVIII. GORDIAN III., a youth of only fifteen years, suceeeded to the Empire by common consent, and his reign displayed courage and moderation. He was undermined, however, by the arts of Philip, the Pretorian Prefect; and the support of the army being withdrawn, he was easily cut off, A. D. 244, having reigned six years.

36. Small silver. Youthful head. IMP. GORDIANUS PIUS FEL(ix) AUG. ℞. Usual titles. 37. Large silver. ℞. LÆTITIA AUG. N. 38, 39. ℞. JOVI STATORI. Figure of Jupiter Stator. 40. ℞. SAECULI FELICITAS.

41. ORIENS AUG. The Emperor flattered as the "rising sun." 42. JOVI CONSERVATORI. "To Jupiter the Preserver." 43. MARS PROPUG(nator). "Mars, the Champion." 44. Usual official titles.

45. L. Brass. SECURITAS PERPET(ua). 46. As No. 38. 47, 48. Silver, of Sabina Tranquillina, Empress; married to Gordian in 241. (No. 48, *cb.*; No. 47 doubtful.)

XXIX. PHILIP, an Arab chief, afterwards a Roman general, proved an excellent ruler, notwithstanding the base means of his promotion; and was in high esteem with the Senate and people. His son, Philip II., though but a child, was associated in the Empire. Their reign, with their lives, was cut short by the successful revolt of the army in Panonia (Austria) under Decius. Philip was killed, A. D. 249, in his forty-sixth year, and sixth of his reign. The younger Philip was aged thirteen.

50. Small silver. IMP. M(arcus) JUL(ius) PHILIPPUS AUG. ℞. The Emperor on horseback; ADVENTUS AUGG. "Arrival of the Emperors." 51. Large silver. ℞. SECURIT(as) ORBIS. "The safety of the world." 52, 53, 54, 55. ℞. SÆCULARES AUGG. These coins severally bear on the *rev.* a lion, a stag, a goat, and a column with COS. III.; and another, of the Empress, bears a hippopotamus. The secular games were celebrated with magnificence, A. D. 247, and third year of Philip, as being the 1000th year of Rome, by the computation of Varro. Other coins of the same date (not in this collection) bear the legend MILLIARUM SÆCULUM, the "millennium" of Rome. 56. ℞. ÆQUITAS AUGG.

57. VIRTUS AUG. 58. An elephant and his rider; ÆTERNITAS AUGG. 59. Base silver. Greek coin of Philip; Antioch in Syria. 60. Brass. ℞. A stag; SÆCULARES AUGG. 61. FELICITAS TEMP(orum). "The happiness of the times." 62. Large silver. OTACIL(ia) SEUERA AUG. ℞. PIETAS AUGUSTÆ. She was married to Philip some years before he became Emperor, and survived him a very short time. She was of pure character, and is said to have professed the new religion, and to have caused her son, the younger Philip, to be baptized. The Emperor was not (as some have affirmed) the first Christian Emperor, but he suppressed the persecutions. 63. Otacilia. ℞. SÆCULARES AUGG. A hippopotamus, with open mouth. The display of wild animals formed a part of these games. 64. Brass. MARCIA OTACIL(ia) SEVERA. ℞. PIETAS AUGUSTÆ. 65. Large silver. M. JUL. PHILIPPUS CÆS. ℞. The young Philip holding a globe and spear; PRINCIPI JUVENT(utis).

66. Base silver. Greek coin of the younger Philip; Antioch in Syria. 67. Brass, of the same. ℞. Imperfect. 68. The same. SÆCULARES AUGG. COS. II. 69. Large silver. IMP. TI(berius) CL(audius) MAR(ius) PACATIANUS AUG. ℞. SALUS AUGG. The name of this usurper is not found in history, but he is referred to this date by another legend (not in this collection), ROMÆ ÆTER. AN. MILL. ET PRIMO. "Year 1001

of eternal Rome." His coins are found only in France. This is one of several instances in which Roman coins discover the omissions of historians. *cb.* 70. Pacatianus. ℞. Hercules in conflict with the lion; VIRTUS AUG. "Courage of the Emperor." *cb.*

XXX. TRAJAN DECIUS, sent to suppress a mutiny in Panonia, placed himself at the head of it; and having vanquished his master, was acknowledged as Emperor. His reign of two years was spent in warring against the Goths and destroying the Christians; the former of whom had become formidable to the state, as the latter had to the state religion. He fell in battle A. D. 251, aged sixty years.

71. Gold. IMP. C. M. Q. TRAIANUS DECIUS AUG. ℞. A figure holding an ensign; GENIUS EXERC. ILLYRICIANI. The Illyrian army promoted him. 72. Silver. ADVENTUS AUG. His arrival at Rome.

73. DACIA. The battle-ground. 74. GEN. ILLYRICI. 75. Brass. PANNONIA. 76. ℞. As No. 71. 77. Gold. HER(ennia) ETRUSCILLA AUG. ℞. PUDICITIA AUG. This Empress is known only by her coins, and by an inscription. 78. Silver; same rev. 79. Brass; same rev.

80. Greek coin of Etruscilla. ℞. SAMION. Island of Samos. 81. Silver. Q. HER(ennius) ETR(uscus) MES(sius) DECIUS NOB(ilis) C(æsar). This prince perished in battle with his father. 82. Brass, of the same.

83. Silver. CN. VALENS HOSTILIANUS QUINTUS AUG. This prince survived his father, was made colleague to Gallus, and died in a few months, either of plague or poison. 84. ℞. SECURITAS AUGG. (This legend seems a sarcasm upon the times, and especially upon this prince.)

XXXI. GALLUS, commanding on the Danube, was proclaimed by his army, and elected by the Senate, successor to Decius. A precarious peace was purchased of the Goths; but the Empire was afflicted with plague and famine. Gallus was killed by his own soldiers when about to march against Æmilian, A. D. 254; having reigned less than three years; and aged forty-seven.

85. Silver. IMP. C. C. VIB. TREB(onianus) GALLUS AUG. ℞. LIBERTAS PUBLICA. 86. ℞. APOLL(ini) SALUTARI. (An appeal to Apollo, the god of physic, to stay the plague.) 87. ℞. VICTORIA AUGG.

88. Brass. ℞. VIRTUS AUGG. 89. Greek coin of Gallus. Antioch in Syria. 90. Silver. IMP. CÆS. VIB. VOLUSIANUS AUG. ℞. CONCORDIA AUGG. Volusian was associated with his father in the Empire, and perished with him. 91. ℞. As No. 88. 92. Brass. ℞. Same as preceding. 93. Silver. IMP. ÆMILIANUS PIUS FELIX AUG. ℞. SPES PUBLICA. Æmilian, a Moor by birth, and governor of Mæsia, having successfully resisted a Persian invasian, was proclaimed Emperor by his troops, and was acknowledged after the death of Gallus, but survived his elevation only three months. 94. Silver. C. CORNELIA SUPERA AUG. ℞. JUNO REGINA. This lady, wife of Æmilian, is known only by her coins. *cb.* 95. ℞. VESTA. *cb.*

XXXII. VALERIAN, of illustrious family and pure character, was promoted to the Empire upon the fall of Gallus and Æmilian, A. D. 254, being then sixty years of age. His troubled reign was terminated in 260, by his being taken prisoner by the King of Persia, in whose hands, after much cruel treatment, he died.

99. Silver. IMP. C. P. LIC(inius) VALERIANUS AUG. ℞. VICTORIA AUGG. 100. ORIENS AUG. 101. DIVI MARINIANA. Wife of Valerian. ℞. A peacock, bearing the departed spirit. CONSECRATIO. 102. ℞. Peacock, with wings outspread. CONSECRATIO. 103. Brass; same as the preceding. 104. Greek coin, brass, of Valerian; Tarsus in Cilicia.

XXXIII. GALLIENUS was adopted into the Empire A. D. 254, at the age of thirty-six; and became sole Emperor upon the captivity of his father, an event which gave him no concern. In this reign, "heaven and earth seemed to concur in heaping afflictions upon the Empire." Usurpers seized upon the fairest provinces, and maintained their ground; the barbarians grew bolder in their irruptions; and the plague, raging everywhere and lingering for years, cut off a vast proportion of the people. Gallienus allowed nothing to interfere with his ease and pleasures, except a campaign against the Germans, and another agaist a rebel general, in which he perished, A. D. 268.

107. Silver. GALLIENUS P. F. AUG. ℞. VICT(oria) GERMANICA. 108. ℞. GERMANICUS MAX(imus). 109. A quinarius. VICTORIA AUG. *cb.* 110. DIVO PIO. Head of Antoninus Pius. (Gallienus caused the issue of a series of coins in billon, bearing the heads of his most eminent predecessors. There is a vast variety of dies in this reign, without any improvement in the art.) 111. Small brass. ℞. JOVI CONSERVATORI. 112. Billon, of Salonina, Empress. 113. ℞. VENUS FILIA.

114. Brass. VESTA. 115. Billon, of Saloninus Valerian, son of Gallienus. ℞. PRINC. JUVENT. 116. ℞. PIETAS AUG. 117. Quinarius. Same reverse. *cb.* 118. A boy riding a goat. JOVI CRESCENTI.

119. Brass, of the same. ℞. A funeral pile.

USURPERS. During the feeble reign of Gallienus, the purple was assumed by about twenty generals, in different parts of the Empire. Most of these were soon overthrown; but there were two extensive monarchies which stood out against Gallienus and his immediate successor. The first, created by the famous Zenobia, Queen of Palmyra, included Syria and Egypt, and lasted six years, 267-73. The other, originated by Postumus, was composed of Gaul, Spain, and Britain, and continued fifteen years, 258-73. All these provinces were eventually restored to Rome by the bravery and address of Aurelian.

POSTUMUS, Governor of Gaul, assumed the title of Emperor, 258; was killed by his troops, 267.

VICTORINUS, a general of Postumus, was associated with him, 265; and was also killed by his soldiers, 267.

LÆLIANUS, competitor of Postumus, was also killed by his own troops.

MARIUS, successor to Victorinus, was killed almost as soon as crowned.

TETRICUS, a Senator, and Governor of Aquitaine, succeeded to this monarchy, and reigned undisturbed six years. In 273, he abdicated with his son; and both retired to Rome for the remainder of their lives. A vast variety of coins was issued by these Emperors, or Usurpers.

120. Plated brass, or copper. IMP. C. POSTUMUS P. F. AUG. ℞. Hercules and Postumus, face to face. FELICITAS AUG. 121. Base silver. Front, face of Postumus. ℞. INDULG(entia) PIA POSTUMI AUG. *cb.* It is uncertain what this "pious indulgence" was. 122. Profile; same ℞. *cb.* 123. Billon. SÆCULI FELICITAS. 124. A quinarius. VICTORIA AUG. *cb.* 125. Billon, or copper; same ℞. 126. PAX AUG.

127. Plated brass. ℞. VIRTUS AUG. 128. ℞. JOVI PROPUGNATORI. 129. Large brass. Heads of Postumus and Hercules side by side, and on the reverse, face to face. *cb.* 130. Plated brass. A woman recumbent, personifying the Rhine; SALUS PROVINCIARUM. "Safety of the provinces." 131. Silver. IMP. C. VICTORINUS P. F. AUG. ℞. VIRTUS AUG. *cb.* 132. Brass, or copper. ℞. PROVIDENTIA AUG.

133. ℞. PAX AUG. 134. Silver, of Marius. ℞. CONCORDIA MILITUM. *cb.* 135. ℞. SÆ(culi) FELICITAS. *cb.* 136. Silver, of Lælianus. ℞. TEMPORUM FELICITAS. *cb.* 137. Gold, of Tetricus the elder. Usual titles. *cb.* 138. Silver. ℞. PAX ÆTERNA. *cb.* 139. Heads of Tetricus senior and junior. ℞. ÆTERNITAS AUGG. *cb.* 140. Copper, of Tetricus senior. PIETAS AUG. 141. SALUS AUG. 142. Gold. C. PES(uvius) TETRICUS CÆSAR. ℞. SPES AUGG. *cb.* 143. Silver. Same reverse. *cb.* 144. Copper. ℞. PIETAS AUGUST(orum). Sacrificial utensils. 145. ℞. SPES PUBLICA. 146. ℞. PRIN. JUVENTUTIS.

XXXIV. CLAUDIUS II., surnamed GOTHICUS, succeeded Gallienus, as the dying choice of that prince, and with the consent of the army and Senate By a brave onset he repulsed the daring Goths, which gained him the above surname. Two years after his accession, and at the age of fifty-five, he was carried off by the plague, A. D. 270.

148. Gold. IMP. CLAUDIUS PIUS FELIX AUG. ℞. VICTORIA AUG. 149. Silver. ℞. PAX EXERC(ituum). *cb.* 150. Small brass. FIDES EXERCIT. 151. ℞. LÆTITIA. 152. Silver, of QUINTILLUS, brother of Claudius, who assumed the Empire upon his death, but retained it only a few days. 153. Small brass, of the same.

DIVISION V.

AURELIAN TO THE END OF THE WESTERN EMPIRE. 270-475.

XXXV. AURELIAN, general of cavalry, succeeded A. D. 270. His reign of five years was employed in clearing the Empire of the numerous foes, foreign and domestic, who had for years been threatening its existence. He was entirely successful, and the Roman rule was everywhere reëstablished. He was a severe disciplinarian, such as the times required; but his severity gave ground for a conspiracy, which cost him his life, A. D. 275. He was over sixty years of age at his death.

3. Middle brass. IMP. AURELIANUS AUG. ℞. CONCORDIA AUG. 4. Small br. ℞. VIRTUS AUG. 5. Small br., of Severina, Empress. ℞. CONCORDIÆ MILITUM.

XXXVI. On the death of Aurelian, a singular contest arose between the army and Senate, each requesting the other to nominate a successor. Six months elapsed in this generous strife; at length the Senate chose TACITUS, one of their own body, seventy-five years old, and of exemplary character. He lived only six months after his elevation. The historian Tacitus was claimed by the Emperor as his ancestor.

10. Brass. IMP. C. M. CL(audius) TACITUS AUG. ℞. FELICIT(as) TEMP(orum). 11. ℞. A woman holding a purse ; UBERITAS. "Plenty." 12. ℞. CONCORDIA MILITUM. 13. Silver, of Florianus, brother of Tacitus, who assumed the purple as successor, but was murdered by his troops, A. D. 276. *cb.* 14. Brass, of the same. VIRTUS AUG.

XXXVII. PROBUS, during a reign of six years, was warring from the Rhine to the Nile, and always with success. In a recess of peace, having set the soldiers to draining a marsh, a mutiny was raised, and he fell, A. D. 282, aged fifty. "In civil and military virtue, he was equal to any predecessor."

17. Gold. IMP. C. M. AUR(elius) PROBUS AUG. ℞. SECURITAS SÆCULI. In the exergue, SIS., for Siscia, either his birthplace, or the place of coinage. 18. Plated brass. ℞. ROMÆ ÆTERNÆ. (He repaired the city.) 19. Small brass. SOLI INVICTO. 20. ℞. VICTORIA GERM. The Germans were driven from Gaul with immense loss ; nine kings submitted, and sixteen thousand German youth were taken into the Roman army.

XXXVIII. CARUS, Pretorian Prefect under Probus, succeeded that prince by election of the army, A. D. 282, at the age of fifty-two. He was killed in his tent by lightning, in a campaign against Persia, about one year after.

26. Brass. IMP. CARUS P. F. AUG. ℞. SPES PUBLICA. P. XXI. 27. ℞. PAX EXERCIT. XXI.

XXXIX. CARINUS and NUMERIAN, sons of Carus, succeeded their father, A. D. 283. The former was plunged in debauchery ; the latter, a virtuous youth, contracted a disease of the eyes in grief for his parent, which obliged him to travel in a close litter. In this hidden place he was murdered by his ambitious father-in-law, Aper, A. D. 284. Carinus also died by violence, a year after.

29. Small brass. M. Aur(elius) Carinus Nob(ilis) C(æsar). ℞. Principi Juvent. 30. Pietas Augg. (These two were struck before the death of Carus.) 31. Washed brass, of Magnia Urbica, a lady known only by her coins, but supposed to be the wife of Carinus. ℞. Venus Genetrix. *cb.* 32. Brass, of the same. ℞. Venus Victrix.

33. Base silver. Divo Nigriniano. This deified youth is supposed to have been a son of Carinus. *cb.* 34. Base silver, of Julianus, usurper. *cb.* 35. Gold. ℞. Aur(elius) Numerianus Nob. C. ℞. Principi Juvent. 36. Silver. ℞. Pietas Augg. *cb.* 37. Brass. Imp. Numerianus Aug. ℞. Pietas Augg. 38. ℞. Providentia Augg. xxi. 39. Brass, same legends as the gold coin.

XL. DIOCLETIAN, a master spirit, though born a slave, received the Empire from the army, A. D. 285, at the age of forty. The next year he associated MAXIMIAN HERCULES; and in 292, the two called to their aid Galerius and Constantius Chlorus, as Cæsars, and the Empire was divided into four jurisdictions; Diocletian in the East, Maximian over Italy and Africa, Galerius in the region between the Adriatic and Euxine, and Constantius in the West. The two Emperors abdicated in 305. This long reign was signalized by the increase of despotism, by incessant wars, and by a systematic effort to root out Christianity.

41. Gold. Diocletianus P. F. Aug. ℞. Jovi Conser. Augg.

42. Silver. ℞. XCVI. Aq. (Struck at Aquileia, in Italy.) 43. ℞. The Emperor and officers sacrificing before a camp. Virtus Militum.

44. Brass. ℞. Jovi Tutatori Augg. "To Jupiter, defender of the Emperors." 45. ℞. Genio Populi Romani. Aq. P. "To the Genius of the Roman People." 46. ℞. Vot. XX., within a wreath.

47. Concordia Militum. 49. Gold. Imp. C. M. A. Maximianus Aug. ℞. Virtuti Herculis. 50. Silver. ℞. Same as No. 44.

51. ℞. As on No. 41. *cb.* 52. Brass. D(omino) N(ostro) Maximiano Beatissimo Sen. Aug. "To our most blessed lord Maximian the elder." 53. ℞. Genio Augg. et Cæsarum N. N. Ka. (Carthage mint.)

54. As No. 47. 55. Imp. Carausius P. F. Aug. ℞. Pax Aug. This remarkable man was a Roman admiral on the coast of Britain. In 287 he seized upon that island, made it an empire for himself, and forced an acknowledgment of his claim by the Roman Emperors. He reigned with *éclat* for six years, when he fell by the hand of his minister Allectus; who was subdued by the forces of Constantius, two years after, 295. (The coins extant of these two usurpers or emperors are comparatively few, although they are of considerable variety in device. This specimen was lately dug up in England.)

XLI. The administration now presents a confused multitude of Augusti and Cæsars. GALERIUS and CONSTANTIUS CHLORUS, succeeding their patrons in 305, Severus and Maximin Daza were called to take part in the government. In 306, the restless Max. Hercules returned to the Empire with his son MAXENTIUS; Severus was made Emperor; Constantius died (in Britain), and his son Constantine took the rank of Cæsar. In 307, Severus died, and LICINIUS became an Emperor. 308, Maximin Daza assumed the purple in the East, and Constantine in the West, so that the Romans now supported the burden of *six* emperors, each with his court and camp. Four of these died or were killed nearly at the same time: Maximian in 310; Galerius, 311; Maxentius, 312; and Maximin Daza, 313. History hesitates to decide which was the greatest tyrant.

58. Silver. Constantius Cæs. ℞. As No. 43. 59. Small brass. ℞. Concordia Militum. 60. Small brass, of Theodora, second wife of Constantius. 62. Silver, of Galerius. Maximianus Nob. C. ℞. A camp; Virtus Militum. 63. Brass. Imp. C. Gal(erius) Val(erius)

Maximianus P. F. Aug. ℞. Genio Imperatoris. 64. ℞. As No. 45. 65. Brass, of Valeria, wife of Galerius. 66. Brass, of Severus. ℞. Salvis Augg. et Cæs. Fel. Kart. 67. Do., of Maximin Daza. ℞. As No. 63. 68. Small brass, of the same. 69. Brass, of Maxentius. ℞. Conserv. Urb. Suæ. "Preserver of his own city." 70. Small brass, of Romulus, infant son of Maxentius.

XLII. CONSTANTINE the Great, succeeding his father in the West in 306, had but one colleague, or competitor, remaining in 313. LICINIUS, his brother-in-law, reigned in the East; and after various collisions and compacts, the latter was forced to yield his throne in 323, and his life the year after. Constantine, remaining sole Emperor, restored peace and solidity to the Empire, built a new capital (Constantinople), and established Christianity as the state religion. He died in 337, at the age of sixty-three.

73. Gold. Constantinus Magnus. ℞. Jupiter standing; Jovi Conservatori Augg. TS. B. This must have been struck before his conversion to Christianity (in 311), or before his open avowal of it.

75. Small brass. ℞. Soli Invicto Comiti. (The sense is obscure.) 76. ℞. A camp; Providentia Augg. 77. ℞. Mars standing; Marti Conservatori.

[There is a rare type extant, not in this collection, bearing the monogram of Christ, and the legend In hoc Signo Vinc(es), the Latin version of *Touto Nika* (Gr.), "By this (sign) conquer." This sign was the appearance of a splendid cross in the heavens, which, as he affirmed some years afterwards, was presented to his view, near Milan, on his march against Maxentius; and to which he attributed both his victory and his conversion. It is remarkable as the introduction of the Christian emblems, which become more and more common, until scarce any thing else appears on the coins. See the series of the Lower Empire.]

78. Silver. Flav(ia) Max(ima) Fausta Aug. ℞. The Empress suckling two infants; Spes Reipublicæ. Sirmium. (She was the daughter of Maximian, sister of Maxentius, and wife of Constantine. Having caused the death of Crispus by a false charge, she was condemned by the Emperor to the same fate, 326, after a union of nineteen years.) *cb.* 79. Small brass, same type. 80. Same figure, with Salus Reipublicæ. 81. Jul(ius) Crispus Nob(ilis) Cæs. ℞. Virtus Exercit. Crispus was the son of Constantine, and a favorite of the army; but was put to death on an accusation of the Empress, his step-mother, 326.

82. ℞. Vict(oriæ) Lætæ Princ. Perp. Siscia. 83. Silver. Fl(avius) Delmatius Nob. Cæs. He was a nephew of Constantine, and governed Greece; killed by the soldiers, 337. *cb.* 84. Small brass, of the same. ℞. Gloria Exercitus. 85. Brass. Imp. Lic(inianus) Licinius P. F. Aug. ℞. As No. 73. 86. Small brass; same reverse. 87. ℞. as No. 75. 88. Small brass, of the younger Licinius. (Put to death, 326, at the age of eleven years.)

XLIII. The Empire now underwent another division and reunion. CONSTANTINE II. had the West; CONSTANS the middle provinces, with Italy; and CONSTANTIUS II. the East. The first fell in a war with his next brother, A. D. 340; the second was overcome by Magnentius, 350; and from the overthrow of that usurper, in 353, Constantius II. remained sole Emperor, finishing a long and inglorious reign in 361, aged forty-four.

89. Gold. No legend around the head. ℞. Constantinus Cæsar. 90. Silver. ℞. Votis XXX. Multis XXXX. Ant. (for the mint at

Antioch.) 91. Small brass. CONSTANTINUS JUNIOR NOB. C. ℞. GLORIA EXERCITUS. 92. ℞. CÆSARUM NOSTRORUM. VOT. V.

93. ℞. Same, with VOT. X. 94. ℞. A camp; PROVIDENTIA CÆSS. 95. Gold. CONSTANS AUGUSTUS. ℞. VICTORIA DD. NN. AUGG. TR. On a shield held by two genii or angels, VOT. X. MULT. XX. See No. 101. 96. Brass. ℞. A soldier holding the military ensign or labarum, on which is the monogram of Christ. FEL(icium) TEMP(orum) REPARATIO. "The restoration of happy times." 97. Small brass. ℞. as No. 95, except the shield. 98. CONSTANTINOPOLIS. Helmeted head, personifying the new city. 99. Gold. FL. JUL. CONSTANTIUS PERP. AUG. ℞. A shield, with VOT. XX. MULT. XXX. Legend, GLORIA REIPUBLICÆ. SMNT. 100. Gold quinarius. ℞. VICTORIA AUGUSTI. VOT. XXX. 101. Silver. ℞. VOTIS XXV. MULTIS XXX. ANT. (This inscription, the style of which now becomes common, is a brief way of saying, that the Emperor has renewed or accomplished his inaugural vow twenty-five times, i. e. has enjoyed the title of Augustus, or Cæsar, for twenty-five years, and it is hoped that he will complete at least as many as thirty; this is the only plausible interpretation of MULT. XXX. It seems but a feeble compliment to a monarch; however, as will be seen by the next coin, as soon as he had accomplished VOTIS XXX., the wish was ready for MULT. XXXX.) 102. ℞. VOTIS XXX. MULTIS XXXX. It must be counted from the time he was created Cæsar by his father, in 323. 103. Brass. A soldier leading a child; FEL. TEMP. REPARATIO. The favorite legend of Constantine's family.

104. ℞. GLORIA ROMANORUM. 105. Sm. brass. CONSTANTIUS JUN NOB. C. ℞. A globe on a pedestal. 106. ℞. GLORIA EXERCITUS.

107. ℞. VOT. XX. MULT. XXX. 108. Silver, of Vetranio, a Roman general and usurper, in Pannonia; reigned ten months. *cb.*

109. Brass, of Magnentius, a more formidable usurper, in Gaul reigned three years, and was subdued, after refusing a share of the Empire offered by Constantius, 353. 110. Sm. brass, of the same.

111. Silver, of Decentius, brother and coadjutor of Magnentius.

112. Large silver, of the same. The Christian symbol behind the head. *cb.*

XLIV. JULIAN, nephew of Constantine the Great, was famous for his efforts to bring back the Empire to paganism, chiefly by his pen. Some real reforms were also brought about in the government and the manners at court. But the desire of figuring as a conqueror led him into Persia, from whence he with difficulty effected a retreat, and on the way lost his life, 363, at the age of thirty-two, and after a reign of two years, counting from the death of Constantius II., or about three from his elevation by the army at Paris.

113. Gold. FL(avius) CL(audius) JULIANUS P. P. AUG. ℞. VIRTUS EXERCITUS ROMANORUM. SIRM. 114. Silver. D(ominus) N(oster) FL., &c. ℞. VOT. X., MULT. XX. Counting from his *Cæsarship.*—The long beard recalls the derision of the citizens of Antioch, where he wintered, and the consequent production of the *Misopogon*, one of the Emperor's literary efforts. 115. Large brass. ℞. The sacred bull Apis; SECURITAS REIPUB(licæ). CONST. Julian was partial to the Egyptian deities. 116. Small brass, of the same. 117. Small brass of Helena, wife of Julian, and sister of Constantius II. SECURITAS REIPUBLICÆ.

XLV. Whilst the generals were in conclave, the soldiers proceeded to elect JOVIAN, a subordinate officer, and a man of no pretensions. He survived his elevation only seven months, A. D. 364. Christianity was restored to imperial favor.

123. Brass. D. N. JOVIANUS P. P. AUG. ℞. VOT. V. MULT. X. SIRM. 124. ℞. The same, except the mint-mark, which is SIS. (When these pieces were struck, the imperial vow for five years was evidently just assumed, not completed; showing that these dates are to be variously understood.)

XLVI. VALENTINIAN I., son of Count Gratian, received the Empire from the army, and at their instance placed his brother VALENS over the Eastern provinces. The tendency towards a division of Rome was thus accelerated. The former died 375, having reigned eleven years; the latter survived him three years, and was burnt to death in a cottage, where he had taken shelter in battle.

129. Gold. Head and titles of Valentinian. ℞. VICTORIA AUGG. TR. OB. 130. Silver. ℞. VOT. X. MULT. XX. ANT. 131. Small brass. ℞. The Christian cipher on a military standard; GLORIA ROMANORUM. SISC. 132. ℞. SECURITAS REIPUBLICÆ. 133. Silver. URBS ROMA. TRPS. 134. Small brass. RESTITUTOR REIPUBLICÆ. SIS.

135. SECURITAS REIPUBLICÆ. 136. Silver, of Procopius, a usurper at Constantinople. *cb.*

XLVII. GRATIAN, a youth, and VALENTINIAN II., a child, succeeded to the throne of their father in the West, 375. On the death of Valens, they associated the famous Theodosius, of Spain, who was stationed in the East. Gratian fell in 383, at the age of twenty-four, while on the march against a usurper in Gaul; his brother perished by the hand of an assassin in 392, aged twenty-one; and the whole Empire remained to Theodosius.

137. Gold. Head and titles of Gratian. ℞. As No. 129.

138. Silver. ℞. URBS ROMA. TR. PS. 139. Brass. ℞. REPARATIO REIPUBLICÆ. P. CON. 140. Small brass. ℞. SECURITAS REIPUBLICÆ. SIS. 141. Brass. D. N. MAGNUS MAXIMUS P. F. AUG. ℞. As on No. 139. A usurper in Gaul, who maintained his power four years, 383–387. 142. Gold. Head and titles of Valentinian, jun. ℞. As No. 129.

143. Brass. ℞. As No. 139. 144. Smallest brass. ℞. SALUS REIPUBLICÆ.

XLVIII. THEODOSIUS I. was called to a participation of the Empire in 379, at the age of thirty-three. He became sole Emperor in 392, and was the last to enjoy that distinction. In 395 he expired, after an illustrious reign, and left the realm to be divided between his two sons.

145. Gold. Head and titles of Theodosius. ℞. As No. 129.

146. Small silver. VOT. MULT. XXXX. 147. Brass. ℞. REPARATIO REIPUB. SIS. 148. ℞. As No. 131. 149. Small brass. CONCORDIA AUGGG. SIS. 150. Brass, of Flacilla, Empress. ℞. A female figure, and the Christian monogram. SALUS REIPUBLICÆ. CONS.

XLIX. From the accession of Honorius, in 395, about eighty years elapsed to the extinction of the Western Empire. The period was marked by a succession of feeble or nominal princes; by the daring inroads of barbarians; the loss, one by one, of the provinces of Britain, Gaul, Spain, and Africa; and finally the establishment of a Gothic monarchy in Italy itself.

153. Gold, of HONORIUS. ℞. As No. 129. (Died in 423.)

154. Silver. ℞. VIRTUS ROMANORUM. (A remarkable legend for the times.) 155. Brass. ℞. Imperfect. 156. Silver, of CONSTANTIUS III., associate of Honorius, for seven months only. *cb.*

158. Silver. JOHN, secretary to Honorius, afterwards a usurper of the throne, 425. *cb.* 159. Gold, of VALENTINIAN III. Placidius. ℞. As No. 129. (425–455.) 160. Silver, of Justa Grata Honoria,

sister of the preceding. ℞. A figure holding a large cross upright; BONO REIPUBLICÆ. CONOB. *cb.* 163. Gold, of SEVERUS III. An Emperor created by Ricimer, a barbarian general in the Roman service, and really at the head of affairs. ℞. As No. 129. (461 - 465.)

166. Silver, of Ælia Euphemia, wife of Anthemius. *cb.* 168. Silver, of OLYBRIUS, Emperor for three months. 472. *cb.* 169. Small gold, of JULIUS NEPOS. ℞. A cross; CONOB. 474. Romulus Augustus, commonly styled AUGUSTULUS, the last, and merely nominal Emperor, was deposed by Odoacer, 475. The Roman Empire in the West is usually considered as ended at this date.

DIVISION VI.

BYZANTINE EMPIRE.

AT the death of Theodosius I., A.D. 395, the Empire was divided between his two sons, Arcadius and Honorius, the former ruling at Constantinople, the latter at Rome. Although no formal or absolute separation between the East and West was intended by this arrangement (for it had often been practised before), yet such was the ultimate effect. It is not easy to mark the extent of the later Roman Empire, either as to time or territory. Even after the imperial line in the West had ceased (A.D. 475), there was more or less recognition of the sovereign authority of the Emperor at Constantinople, by the barbaric kings, and the popes, in Italy; and Justinian (A.D. 534 - 553), by his renowned generals, Belisarius and Narses, vindicated his title to that region, and to Africa. The crowning of Charlemagne at Rome, A.D. 800, and his proclamation as Emperor of the West* by Pope Leo III., seems to be the most decided limitation of the power of the Eastern Emperor, and a proper commencement for the distinctive name of "*Byzantine*," "*Eastern*," or "*Lower*" Empire. But, as the authority of the monarch at Constantinople was, on the whole, but feebly acknowledged, and more feebly felt, west of the Adriatic Sea, from the time of the division as above stated (395), there is a propriety in dating the Byzantine Empire from that event; and a mixture of unfitness in still designating it, as all historians and numismatists do, as the Roman Empire. This is especially realized as we descend to the last days of the Greek dynasty, and find scarce any part of the immense dominion left, except its trembling capital. But the conquest of Constantinople by the Turks, in 1453, affords an undisputed resting-point.

The coins of this division, if of no interest as works of art, farther than to prove the extreme degeneracy of taste and skill, are equal to any as curiosities, and as illustrations of history.

---

* This title has precariously descended almost to our own day. When the Emperor of Germany changed his title to Emperor of Austria (A. D. 1804), he dropped the old honorary suffix, *Romanus Imperator.* But historians scarcely speak of the Roman Empire as properly continued under the successors of Charlemagne.

Although the series takes in eight centuries of time, there is a general similarity of tone, especially if we start with the second Theodosius; so that one may be sure, by a casual glance at any of them, that it is Byzantine, and not Roman proper. However, they fairly admit of subdivision, and it is not a forced coincidence which places the line at A. D. 811, about midway in the whole series.*

Previous to Michael I. (811-813), we have these peculiarities. On the gold and silver (there is but little of the latter) we have the Emperor, head and bust, and always front face; on the reverse, the monotonous and unjustifiable VICTORIA AUG., at least not justifiable in any other sense than that the Augustus had triumphed over his predecessor. Within this legend, on a high throne, the cross stands conspicuous and erect. As for the copper coins, there is not much variation from the colossal and unintelligible M, K, or I, occupying the field of the reverse. Occasionally, when the imperial power was divided, a number of heads or figures were crowded upon the coin, on both sides.

But from the accession of Michael Rhangabe, we observe a new phase in the coinage, and a more decided display of religious sentiment. The bust or full length of Christ, signalized by the nimbus and legend IHSЧS XPISTЧS, NICA(tor), or REX REGNANTIЧM, or bASILEЧS bASILE(on), expressive of his preëminence as Conqueror, and King of kings, generally occupies one side of the gold and silver coins; on the reverse, the Emperor is sometimes alone, and sometimes shares the space with the Virgin, MHP ΘY, (Mater Theou, "Mother of God,") the two holding aloft, and between them, the standard of the cross. The imperial heads or faces, which in the former series seemed to follow the usual human outline, are here fantastically compressed into triangles or trapeziums. As we near the crusading era, the figures are nearly all at full length, standing or sitting. The legends also have completed the transition from the Latin language to the Greek. On the copper, the vast letters M, K, &c., are nearly superseded by inscriptions, to the same effect as above cited, occupying the field. It is remarkable, however, that while the reading on the copper is quite conspicuous and distinct, that of the gold and silver is so affectedly minute, that a modern eye can scarcely make it out without a magnifier.

(It should be here explained, that we continue the use of the numismatic term *brass*, in the lower coinage, although *copper* seems to be more proper, in every case.)

8. Gold, of ARCADIUS, Emperor. **395-408.** VICTORIA AUGGG. 9. Silver. ℞. VIRTUS ROMANORUM. **10, 11.** Middle brass. GLORIA ROMANORUM. **12.** Small br. VIRTUS EXERCITI. **13.** Very small br.

* That is, by leaving off at about A. D. 1300; there are no coins certainly known later than Andronicus II., who reigned 1282-1328.

The coincidence is more remarkable in another respect. The war against the use of images, which agitated both church and state from the time of the edict of Leo the Isaurian, 726, was brought to an end about 800, by the defeat of the Iconoclasts. The renewed worship or veneration of images was, no doubt. one cause of the marked change in the devices of the coinage, as stated further on.

SALUS REIPUB. 15. Gold, of THEODOSIUS II., son of Arcadius, and Emperor. 408-450. IMP. XXXXII. COS. XVII. P. P.

16. Small br. CONCORDIA AUGG. Expresses a season of harmony between the Eastern and Western Emperors. 17. Gold, of MARCIAN. 450-457. ℞. as No. 8. 18. Gold. LEO I. 457-474. The usual ℞. VICTORIA AUGG. 19. Gold. ZENO. 474-491. 20. Gold. ANASTASIUS. 491-518. 22. Large brass. M. 23. Middle br. K. E. 24. Small br. K. 25. Very small br. I. By this series, the mysterious initials, already mentioned, would seem to stand for denominations of coin; but some subsequent instances rather oppose this inference. 26. Gold, of JUSTIN I. 518-527. 27, 28, 29. Large and middle brasses, of the same. 30. Gold, of JUSTINIAN I. 527-565. (Died at the age of 82.) 31, 32, 33. Large and middle brasses of the same; ANNO XIIII — XVI — XVIIII. They do not answer to our preconceptions of the era of the Civil Code and Pandects.

34. Small silver coin of GELIMAR, king of the Vandals in Africa. (His kingdom was overthrown, and himself captured, by Belisarius, A. D. 534. He was honorably treated, and provided for, by Justinian.) D. N. RX. GELIMA. Head of the prince. 36. Gold, of JUSTIN II. 565-578. 37, 38. Large brass of Justin, with Sophia, Empress.

39. Large br., of TIBERIUS II. ANNO VI. 578-582. 40. Gold, of MAURICE. 582-602. 41, 42. Large and small br., of the same. ANNO X. — IIII. 43. Gold, of FOCAS (as it is on the coins), usually spelt Phocas. 602-610. 44. Large br., of the same. 45. Middle br., Phocas, and Leontia, Empress. 46. Gold, of HERACLIUS I. 610-640. Heads of the Emperor and son. 47. Large silver, of the same. (Weighs 100 grs.) 48, 49, 50. Large and middle brasses, of the same. 51. Silver, of CONSTANS II. 641-668. 52. Gold, of CONSTANTINE IV., surnamed POGONATUS, on account of his beard, which is conspicuous. 668-685. 53. Sm. brass, of the same.

54. Gold, of JUSTINIAN II. 685-711. The loss of his nose, with his throne, occasioned the surname of RHINOTMETUS. 57. Gold, of ANASTASIUS II. 713-716. 58, 59, 60. Small brasses of LEO III., the Isaurian. 717-741. 61. Gold, of MICHAEL I. Rhangabe. 811-813. ℞. Head of Christ; ıHSYS XRISTOS. 62. Pale gold; the same head, with IC. XC. 63. Large brass, of MICHAEL II., with Theophilus. 820-829. 64. Gold, of THEOPHILUS. 829-842. ℞. Heads of his sons. 65, 66. Large brass, of the same.

67. Gold, of BASIL I. 866-886. ℞. Figure of Christ, sitting; ıhs XRS REX REGNATIHM. (The spelling of those times was not critically exact.) 68. Middle brass, of Basil and his sons. 69, 70. Middle br., of LEO VI., surnamed the Wise. 886-911. ℞. LEOh Eh ΘEO BASILEʋS ROMEOh. "Leo, in (or under) God, King of the Romans." *Basileus* was then considered an equivalent to *Imperator* or *Autocrator*.

71. Middle brass, of Leo and his brother Alexander. LEOh S. ALEXAhGROS (so spelt) BASIL. ROMEOh. This, as in the previous coin, is an inscription, spread over the whole reverse of the piece.

72. Gold, of ROMANUS I., with his son Christophorus. 919-944. 73. Gold, of CONSTANTINE X., with his son Romanus II. 911-

959. A part of the time he was colleague with Romanus I. 74. Middle br., of Constantine alone. 75. Same, of Constantine, and his mother Zoë. 76, Same, of ROMANUS II. 959-963. ℞. As No. 69.

78. Gold, of NICEPHORUS II. PHOCAS. 963-969. See frontispiece, No. 4. 79, 80, 81. Large brasses, of JOHN ZIMISCES. 969-975. Large inscriptions on the rev., of "Jesus Christ, King of kings," with slight variety. 82. Same. IC. XC. NI KA., arranged in the four angles of a cross. "Jesus Christ, the Conqueror." 85. Large thin silver, of CONSTANTINE XII. Monomachus. 1042-1054. ℞. The Virgin standing with uplifted hands. 86. Gold, of ROMANUS IV. 1068-1071. The Emperor and Virgin standing side by side; the latter with her hand on the Emperor's head. ℞. Christ, seated.

87. Gold, of the same, and nearly the same devices. 88. Pale gold, concave, or "incuse." Michael VII. 1071-1078. 89. Pale gold, incuse. NICEPHORUS III. Botoniates. 1078-1081. The Emperor at full length, holding the globe and labarum. 90. Same, in gold, except the Emperor in *half*-length. 92. Gold, of ALEXIUS I. Comnenus. 1081-1118. ΑΛΕΧΙω. ΔΕCπΟΤ. Τω. ΚΟΜΝΗΜΟ. "Alexius Comnenus, despot." 93. Gold, of the same. ℞. Figure of Christ seated, as if in the act of teaching; holding in one hand the Sacred Scriptures, the other hand uplifted. IC. XC. 95. Gold, of JOHN II. Comnenus, surnamed the Handsome. 1118-1143.

96. Gold, of MANUEL I. Comnenus, surnamed Porphyrogenitus, "Born to the purple." 1143-1180. (It was somewhat a rare honor to be born to a reigning Emperor, and actually to succeed him, the two conditions requisite to this title, which occurs in several instances.)

97, 98. Silver, of the same. 99, 100. Small br., of the same.

101. Middle br., ANDRONICUS I. 1183-1185. 102. Small br., ISAAC II. Angelus. 1185-1203. 103, 104. Coins in middle brass, bearing the head of Christ, with IC. XC. on one side, and an ornamented cross on the other; they are believed to be of the brief dynasty of Latin princes, or Crusaders, who turned aside from their way to Jerusalem, A. D. 1203, to capture Constantinople. They retained the Byzantine Empire, or a large part of it, near sixty years. The throne was restored to the Greek dynasty by the victories of Michael VIII. Paleologus, A. D. 1261. 106. Pale gold, of ANDRONICUS II. Paleologus. 1282-1328. ℞. The Virgin, with uplifted hands, surrounded by the walls of Constantinople.

107, 108, 109. Small silver, doubtfully ascribed to John V. and John VIII., the latter of whom died A. D. 1448, five years before the final triumph of the Turks. 113. A leaden seal, of the Byzantine Empire.

GREEK COINS.

The second general division of antique coins is the *Greek*. The invention of coinage belongs to the Greeks; and by them it was carried to as great perfection as was attained in ancient times. The date of the invention, as well as the exact locality, is uncertain; but it is most probable that coined money was not known earlier than seven centuries before the Christian era.

The coins of this division comprise not only those of Greece and her colonies, but of those countries which were overrun by the Macedonian conqueror, and over whom Greek generals established themselves and their successors. Hence they include Greece proper, Sicily, Southern Italy, and more western points in Europe, and Asia Minor, Syria, Egypt, Persia, and Bactria, during all that time in which the Grecian name was most illustrious in the world, and the Roman was preparing to supplant it.

They are easily subdivided into the Republics and Monarchies.

Of the first sort, there seem to have been not less than *one thousand* cities, colonies, and petty states, who coined their own money, and left an endless, perhaps useless, study for modern antiquarians. Many of them are interesting, but we consider them sufficiently represented in our moderate collection.

In the second class, it has been found necessary to include a few which are not inscribed with Greek characters, nor are in any sense Grecian; such as the daric, the shekel, the fire-worship series of Persia, the barbarian coins of Bactria: they were not sufficient, nor sufficiently congruous, to form a third general division.

GREEK REPUBLICS.

1. ABYDOS. Silv. 2. ACHAIA. Silv. 3. ÆGEA. Silv.

4, 5, 6. ÆGINA. Silv. Three sizes; the largest weighs 170 grs., and is worn; the smallest 13 grs. Ægina had a different standard from most other parts of Greece. The device of a *tortoise* is emblematic of the island, lying securely in the water. The large and small pieces, having no reverse except the marks of the stake on which they were laid in coining, are believed to date near the origin of the art, and may be twenty-five hundred years old. The middle piece seems of a later era. 7. ÆZANIS. Br. 8. AGRIGENTUM. Silv. 9. Do. Br.

10. ALEXANDRIA, of the Troad. Br. 12. AMASIA. Br.

14. AMISUS. Silv. 15. AMPHIPOLIS. Silv. This specimen weighs but seven grains; value less than two cents. A small morsel, to be handed down so many centuries. 16 to 19. APOLLONIA. Silv.

20. ARADUS. Silv. 25. ARGOS, Acarnania. Silv. 26. Do. Peloponnesus. Silv. 28. ATHENS. Silver, tetradrachm; weighs 266 grs.; value about 68 cents. Obverse, a head of Minerva, of very

ancient style; reverse, a large owl, with the letters Α Θ Ε, initials of Athens. The devices are in the boldest relief, and the general style of the coin, coupled with historical facts, indicates an age of twenty-one to twenty-three centuries.

The proverbial saying of the Greeks, "taking owls to Athens," was of the same import as the modern one of "carrying coals to Newcastle" (or, as we should say, to Pottsville).

29. Electrotype copy of the reverse of No. 28. 30, 31. ATHENS. Br. 33. BEREA. Br. 34. BLAUNDOS. Br. 35. BŒOTIA. Silv.

36. BRUTTII. Br. 37. CAMPANIA, Syria. Br. 38. CATANA. *cb.* Silv. 39. CHALCIS, of Eubœa. Silv. 40. Do., of Macedonia. Br. 42. CHERSONESUS TAURICA. Silv. 43. CLAZOMENE. Br. 44. CNOSUS, of Crete. Br. The reverse shows a ground-plan of the famous *labyrinth.* 46. CORCYRA magna. Silv.

49-54. CORCYRA nigra. Br. 57-61. CORINTH. Silv. No. 57, tetradrachm, is of beautiful workmanship. Obverse, head of Minerva; reverse, Pegasus, or the winged horse. 62. CORINTH. Br.

63. COTIACUM. Br. 64. CYRENE. Br. 65. CYZICUS. Br.

66, 67, 68. DYRRACHIUM. Silv. 69. Do. Br. 70. EPHESUS, Ionia. Silv. 71. EPIRUS. Silv. 73. EUBŒA. Silv. 74. GELAS, Silv. 75. Do. Br. 76. HERACLEA, of Lucania. Silv. 78. Do., of Macedonia. Silv. 80. HISTRŒA. Silv. 81. ILISTŒA. Silv.

82. ISTRUS. Silv. 83. LARISSA. Silv. 84. LAMPSACUS. Br.

85. LESBOS. Silv. 86. LETE. Silv. 87. LOCRI. Silv.

88. LOCRI. Br. 89. LEUCADIA. Br. 91, 92, MACEDONIA. Silv. 93. MAMERTINI. Br. 94. MARONEA. Silv. 95. Do. Br.

97, 98, 99. MASSILIA. Silv. These are interesting, as belonging to a colony of Greeks who, to escape the oppressions of a Persian governor, emigrated to the coast of Gaul (about six hundred years before Christ), and settled upon the spot now known as *Marseilles.* The finished workmanship attests their civilization; in which respect they are said to have exerted great influence upon the surrounding Gauls.

100. MILETUS. Br. 101. MYCONUS. Br. 102. MYSIA. Br.

103, 104. NEAPOLIS, of Campania (Naples). Silv. 105, 106, 107. Do. Br. 108. NEAPOLIS, Macedonia. Silv. 110. NEMAUSUS, Greek colony in France; now *Nismes.* Obverse, bears the heads of Augustus and Agrippa, in whose day this was struck.

111. OENIADÆ. Br. 113. PÆSTUM. Br. 115. PANORMUS. Br. 116. PARIUM. Silv. 117. PELLE. Br. 118. PERGAMUS. Silv. 119. PHARSALIA. Silv. 120. PHARUS. Br.

121. PHOCIDIS. Silv. 122. PHŒNIA. Br. 123. PYTOPOLIS. Silv. 124. RHEGIUM. Silv. 126, 127. RHODES. Silv.

128. RHODES. Br. 129. SARDIS. Br. 130. SICYON, island. Silv. 131. Do., Achaia. Silv. 133. SIDE. Silv.

134, 135. SIPHNUS. Silv. 136. Do. Br. 138. SMYRNA. Br.

139. SYRACUSE. Silv. 140. Do. Br. 141. TARENTUM. Silv.

142, 143. TAUROMENIUM. Br. 146. TEANUM. Br.

147. TENEDOS, of the Troad. Br. 148. THASUS. Silv.

149. THESSALY. Silv. 150. THESSALONICA. Silv.

153, 154. THRACE. Silv. 157, 158. VELIA. Silv.

GREEK MONARCHIES.

MACEDON.

THIS kingdom was founded about eight hundred years before Christ; four hundred and fifty years later, it was enlarged by the conquests of Philip, and became still more conspicuous from the military career of his son, Alexander the Great. But the kingdom began to decline at his death, and at length, B.C. 148, became a province of the Roman Empire.

9. Small silver coin, of one of the early kings, uncertain which, but evidently earlier than Alexander I., who flourished about B.C. 500. It bears the Macedonian horse on the obverse, and there is no reverse except the punch-marks. 10, 11. Bronze coins of AMYNTAS II. B.C. 398 – 371.

12. Gold stater of PHILIP II. B.C. 371 – 336. 13. Silver tetradrachm, of the same. 14. Hemidrachm, of the same. 15. Bronze coin, of the same.

17. Gold stater of ALEXANDER III. (THE GREAT.) B.C. 336 – 323. Obverse, head of Minerva; reverse, a female figure, with wings, representing Victory, and bearing a trident. 18, 19. Tetradrachms of the same. The head represents Hercules, clothed with the lion's skin; but it is believed that a likeness of Alexander is also intended. Reverse, figure of Jupiter seated, holding an eagle. Legend, ΑΛΕΞΑΝΔΡΟΥ. "(Money) of Alexander."

Alexander was so jealous of his personal appearance, as to allow the imitation of it, in painting, sculpture, or engraving by only three of his best artists; all *mediocre* hands were strictly forbidden to attempt it.

The lion's skin is said to have been displayed, as showing the descent of the Macedonian royal line, by Caraunus, from Hercules. It is curiously alluded to by the Emperor Constantine VI., Porphyrogenitus, writing in the tenth Christian century. "The kings of Macedonia, instead of the crown, the diadem, and the purple, bear [upon their effigy] the skin of a lion's head. More honorable to them is this than to be decked with pearls and precious stones."

20, 21, 22. Drachms, of the same. (No. 22 has a ring, and appears to have been worn as a pendent ornament; but how long ago is uncertain. Its being a fashion among the Oriental ladies of the present day is some proof that it was also the custom a thousand years ago, as the fashions there are said to undergo but little change.) 23. Drachm, of PHILIP III., brother of Alexander. B.C. 323 – 316.

25, 26. Bronze coins, of CASSANDER. B.C. 316 – 299. 27. Bronze, of PHILIP IV. B.C. 298. 28. Silver, of ALEXANDER IV. B.C. 298 – 294. 29, 30. Bronze, of the same.

31 – 36. Bronze, of ANTIGONUS I. B.C. 279 – 243.

37. Tetradrachm, of PHILIP V. Died B.C. 179.

This piece is so remarkably brittle, that a slight fall broke it; yet, upon assay of a fragment, it was found to be 97 per cent. fine.

38. Bronze coin, of PERSEUS. B.C. 179 – 168. He was taken by the Romans, and was the last king of Macedon.

39. Small bronze; uncertain whose.

PERSIA.

THE ancient coins of the Persian Empire are divisible into three classes. 1. The earliest is that of the dynasty of Cyrus, which began B. C. 560, and ended with Darius III., B. C. 331, by the conquests of Alexander of Macedon. The first coinage is attributed to Darius I., who ascended the throne B. C. 521; from whose name the coins, whether of gold or silver, are usually called *darics;* but they cannot now be assigned to any particular monarch. 2. The second series commences with the Greek domination. In the partition of the vast conquests of Alexander, Syria, Persia, and Bactria constituted one empire, under Seleucus, a Greek general. But at the end of half a century, Persia was erected into a separate monarchy by Arsaces, founder of the dynasty of Arsacidæ, which lasted from B. C. 256 to A. D. 223. The coins of this class bear inscriptions in Greek. 3. The rule of the Greeks was overthrown by Ardeshir, or Artaxerxes, a Persian, A. D. 223 - 226, the first of a new line of monarchs (called *Sassanides*, from Sassan, the father of Ardeshir), who maintained the throne until A. D. 637, when Persia became a part of the empire of the Caliphs. The coins of this third division are in the ancient Persian or Pehlevi character and language, which, along with the worship of fire, were diligently restored by this native dynasty.

41. Silver daric. Obverse, the figure of an archer; reverse, the marks of the stake on which the piece lay in coining. The weight is 83½ grs.; the fineness (by sp. gr. of two specimens) varies from 60 to 80 per cent. There is no legend. The style of the coin indicates a high antiquity.

43. Silver drachm, of Mithridates I., of the Arsacian line; B. C. 156 - 134. The reverses of the Greek series are very similar, and generally to this effect: "The great and illustrious Arsaces, king of kings, and friend of the Greeks." (*Arsaces* was the official name of every monarch of that line.)

44. Drachm of PHRAATES II. B. C. 134 - 129. 45, 46, 47. Drachms, of PHRAATES III. B. C. 70 - 61.

52. Potin (large size), of PHRAATES IV. B. C. 30 - A. D. 13.

54. Drachm, of GOTZARES, A. D. 45 - 48.

The foregoing are in a fair style of work, though inferior to the coins of the other Greek dynasties, especially of Syria and Egypt. The later specimens of the Arsacian line (of which we have a few, for temporary examination only) are very barbarous, indicating more attention to arms than to arts. Such is a specimen of Vologeses III., *alias* Arsaces XXVIII., about A. D. 190.

57 - 67. Silver coins of the Sassanian kings. A. D. 223 - 637.

The legends, although they have engaged the attention of the best numismatists, and that for a long period, cannot be satisfactorily made out; only the name of *Shahpur* (Sapor) can sometimes be discerned. The reverse bears an altar, on which a fire is burning, attended by two magi, or priests. The earliest specimens are of good workmanship, in a bold style; but the devices of later times present little else than a confused jumble of lines. The silver appears to be of good quality; the coins are remarkably *thin*, as compared with the Greek.

EGYPT.

This ancient realm had no coined money anterior to the Greek kings, a dynasty which resulted from the conquest by Alexander of Macedon, and began at his death. From the accession of Ptolemy I. to the death of the last Cleopatra (B. C. 323 to B. C. 30) is a period of two hundred and ninety-three years, interesting to the numismatist as well as to the historian.

73. Silver tetradrachm of Ptolemy II., Philadelphus. B. C. 284 – 246. 74 – 78. Bronze coins of the Ptolemies, uncertain which. No. 74 is an enormous coin, weighing over three ounces. 79. Bronze, of Cleopatra, mother of Ptolemy VIII. 80. Bronze, of Ptolemy VIII. B. C. 116 – 106. 81. Bronze, of Cleopatra, wife of Mark Antony; killed herself, B. C. 30. Egypt then became a province of the Roman Empire.

SYRIA.

Seleucus, surnamed Nicator (conqueror), was the founder of the Grecian dynasty, called after his name the *Seleucidæ*, which ruled in Syria, B. C. 312 to B. C. 65. (See under *Persia.*) The coins of this series are for the most part in the best style of Greek workmanship; the legends are simple and easily read.

89. Silver tetradrachm, of Antiochus Soter, son of Seleucus; B. C. 280 - 261. 90. Do., of Antiochus the Great, B. C. 223 - 187. 91. Do., of Seleucus, son of the preceding. B. C. 187 - 175. 92. Do., of Antiochus Epiphanes, also a son of Antiochus the Great, and famous for his wars with the Jews. B. C. 175 - 164. 93. Bronze coin of the same. The face bearded. 94. Tetradrachm, of Demetrius Soter. B. C. 162 - 150. 95. Drachm, of Alexander Balas. B. C. 150 - 146.

96. Tetradrachm of Demetrius II., Nicator. B. C. 146 - 144.

97. Drachm of Antiochus Dionysius. B. C. 143. 98. Tetradrachm of Antiochus Sidetes. B. C. 139 - 130. 99. Do., of Antiochus Grypus. B. C. 124 - 97. 100. Do., of Philip, B. C. 93 - 86; twenty-first king of this dynasty, and the last but two. — Syria was subdued by Pompey, and made a Roman province, B. C. 65.

101. Jewish shekel, of Simon Maccabeus, who flourished about 145 B. C. The legends are in the Samaritan character; on one side is the budding rod of Aaron, with "*Jerusalem the holy*"; on the other, a cup of incense, or pot of manna, and the legend "*Shekel of Israel.*" The weight is 217 grs.; the fineness (by sp. gr.) about 95 per cent.; consequent value, fifty-five and a half cents. This specimen is one of the rarest and most remarkable in the collection. It is in fine preservation.

102. A copy of the foregoing (made here) to show the reverse side.

103. A shekel with similar devices, the legends being in the Hebrew

character. It is well known to be an invention, and is but a few centuries old. It weighs 197 grs.

This specimen was presented to the collection by the Bank of Pennsylvania. It had lain in the Branch Bank at Lancaster, sewed up in a buckskin cover, for many years; but no one knew how long, nor by whom it was deposited there. It is curious even as a fabrication. It is engraved in the old standard European books on ancient coins.

104. Copy of the preceding (made here), showing the reverse.

LESSER MONARCHIES OF GREECE, ASIA MINOR, ETC.

105. Gold stater, of LYSIMACHUS, King of Thrace. B. C. 320.

106. Silver tetradrachm, of the same. 107. Drachm, of the same

108. Brass, of RHŒMETALCES, King of Thrace; Augustus Cæsar on the reverse. 109. Brass, of PATRÆUS, King of Pronia. 110, 111. Do., of ALEXANDER II., of Epirus. 112. Do., of ABGARUS, King of Edessa. 113. Do., of AGATHOCLES, of Sicily. 114. Drachm, of PHILISTIS. *cb.*

115. Brass, of HIERO II. 116. Do., of PHINTIAS. 117. Denarius of JUBA I., King of Numidia. 118. Brass, of COTYS II., Bosphorus.

119. Brass, of PRUSIAS I., King of Bithynia. 121, 122. Do., of PRUSIAS II.

124. Drachm of ARIARATHES VII., King of Cappadocia. 125. Do., of ARIOBARZANES III.

126. Small brass, of AGRIPPA II., of Judea. A. D. 48.

BACTRIA (NOW BOKHARA AND CABUL).

THIS remote Greek monarchy was founded about B. C. 250, by a secession from the great Syro-Persian Empire.

A large number of the coins of Bactria and adjacent regions were lately discovered by British officers in the service of the East India Company. The details of the manner, and the localities, in which they were found, may be seen in the recent work of Prof. Wilson, on the "Antiquities and Coins of Afghanistan"; where they are also fully and admirably illustrated.

137, 138. Large and small brass (or copper), of EUKRATIDES, about B. C. 180. 139. Silver, of ANTIMACHUS, B. C. 140. 140 - 143. Silver, of MENANDER, B. C. 126. 144. Brass, of the same. 145. Brass, of AGATHOKLES, who attempted to form a new monarchy, B. C. 135.

146. Silver, of APOLLODOTUS, B. C. 110. 147, 148. Brass, of the same. 149. Silver, of HERMÆUS, B. C. 98. 150, 151. Brass, of the same. — After this dynasty came a succession of Barbarian and Indo-Scythian princes, whose history is still more scanty and obscure.

153. Brass, of AZES, B. C. 50. 154, 155, 156. Brass, of SOTER MEGAS, "the Great Deliverer," — name unknown. B. C. ——.

157 - 160. Brass, of KADPHISES, supposed about A. D. 100.

161 - 165. Brass, of KANERKES, date unknown, but supposed not later than A. D. 300. 169, 170. Silver coins of Rajpoot princes, not later than A. D. 1200. 171 - 174. Silver Hindu coins, of the Middle Ages.

MODERN COINS.

THE subject of modern coins having been already largely discussed, in a recent work by the Assayers of this Mint, it will only be necessary here to call attention to a few of the more curious specimens.

UNITED STATES. In this series we have the interesting suite of Massachusetts silver coins, of the date of 1652; the silver coins of Cecil, Lord Baltimore, struck about ten years later; the Colonial brass coins of the Carolinas, and the copper of Virginia; the variety of copper coins struck by the States after the treaty of peace, and before the adoption of the Constitution; a very remarkable gold coin, equal in value to a doubloon, coined at New York in 1787; the Washington cent of 1791, of two varieties or reverses, (coined by one Hancock at Birmingham, in England, but at whose instance cannot be ascertained; it was, however, disapproved of), and a larger copper coin, bearing the head of Washington and the date of 1792, from a die which was also used in restamping half-crowns, the enterprise of some individual.* Next come the trial-pieces of the infant national mint; among which, as it was patronized by the President, though not actually coined in the mint, may be counted the "half-disme," bearing the legend, "Liberty, Parent of Science and Industry." In 1794, the mint began to be in regular operation; and we have specimens (though the series is not complete) of the mintage of every year. There is a little variation in the devices of the coins as far as to 1808; but from that date to 1834 (excepting a change in the quarter-dollar, in 1833) there is an undisturbed uniformity, which, if it be desirable in a commercial view, makes but a dull exhibition. At that time, however, the standard of the gold coin was changed, and a modification of device became necessary; and after the public taste had recovered from its alarm at the removal of "E pluribus unum," it was less difficult to progress in the path of change and improvement. The year 1836 was remarkable for new patterns and projects. It was supposed that Liberty might be symbolized by other forms than the matronly bust, and that the eagle might change its perch. Hence we have the famous new dollar of that year. There was also produced, obedient to calls of committees of Congress, the gold dollar, and the two-cent billon piece, the latter being a mixture in which two cents' worth of silver was contained, or lost, in a sizable proportion of copper; but neither was approved. Further varieties, especially in the half-dollar, appear in 1837; and in 1838 there are a number of half-dollar trial-pieces, none of which were adopted. In that year the gold eagle reappears; and all the gold coin is in a new dress. The silver dollars continue very scarce until 1840, when the flying eagle is discontinued; and the entire coinage remains unaltered from that date to the present. (Some material changes are, however, in contemplation.)

---

* We have some other copper coins, of various sizes, bearing the head of Washington, but as they are evidently mere fancy-pieces, of private issue, it has not been thought worth while to give them a place among the authorized coins.

At the end of the United States series are placed specimens of the private gold coinage of Bechtler, of North Carolina, and Reid, of Georgia; the former is still carried on. There are also the silver coins of Chalmers, of Annapolis, 1783, and a guinea restruck with the die "Immune Columbia," and bearing the same date.

Great Britain. The coins of this country are generally considered as the next in interest to our own, by American collectors. Our series is far from being complete, though it contains a number of interesting and rare pieces. The most remarkable in gold are the noble of Henry VI.; ryal of Elizabeth; (this fine, broad piece, in perfect preservation, was selected from a deposit for recoinage, and of course cost only its bullion value;) five-guinea piece of Charles II., value $25.35; and five-pound piece of George IV., 1826, of exquisite workmanship. Of silver coins, we have a few Saxon and early Norman pennies (those of William the Conqueror being of the number dug up at Beaworth, Hampshire, in 1833; they are of various mints, and in the best preservation); also a tolerable succession of silver coins down to Anne, from whose time both gold and silver are sufficiently complete. We have but few copper coins, except from George III. downward. The curious series of copper tokens issued about the close of the last century, and of silver ones current during the suspension of specie payments, dating 1804-1815, are tolerably complete.

France. Of French coins we have one, of the Merovingian line, very rare; the only one older than the base silver of Charles VIII., 1483-1498; the series is pretty full from about 1700.

Germany. The gold ducat of the Emperor Frederick IV., 1452-1493, is our oldest coin; there are a good many of the seventeenth century, and a good collection of those since 1700. As every petty state and free city coins its own money, their number being also greater in former times than at present, the collection and discrimination of German specimens is, or may be made, an interminable business.

About fifty gold coins, generally ducats and halves, in perfect order, came in one parcel for recoinage, and were rescued from the furnace. They are old and curious; some of them being marriage and baptismal tokens, with piquant verses in German; as, for instance, one on which the ceremony of baptism is portrayed, and under it the legend, *Dis Wasser bad, Gibt heil und gnad:* "This water-bath gives holiness and grace." One of the pieces, from its symbols, appears to be a medal of the secret order of Rosicrucians. (These coins are in the large case.)

Portugal. Here is the five-moidore piece of 1725, worth $32.70; the largest of gold coins. There is a good series of *Joannese*, or "half-joes," formerly well known in our currency; the silver and copper are also well represented. The same is true of the kindred series of Brazil, in the same case.

Spain. All those coins which were struck in America, though bearing royal insignia, are to be found in the case labelled "Spanish-American." There is a good modern series of Spanish proper. Two dollars, siege-pieces of 1808-1809, are remarkable.

RUSSIA. The gold half-rouble, worth only 37 cents, the platina coins, and the immense copper pieces, here attract most notice.

TUSCANY, ETC. The silver coins of the Medici family, from 1575 downward, were obtained as bullion, and are in fine keeping. — A scudo of Paul V., 1620, is our oldest Papal coin. — We have, among the Neapolitan, the coins of Joseph Napoleon and Joachim Murat, which, though recent, are scarce.

The SPANISH AMERICAN suite is very full, and well preserved. Here are all the varieties of the famous gold *doubloon* and silver *dollar*. (The quarter cob-doubloon, No. 5, an old piece, was lately picked up by a schoolboy, on a heap of rubbish, near Fairmount; and, from its appearance at the time, was taken for a bit of iron. It may have lain there half a century.)

The OTTOMAN collection represents nearly every reign, from that of Murad I., who died in 1389.

Of the ASIATIC coins, attention will be given to the gold toman of Bokhara, a very inaccessible sort of coin; the bullet-shaped *tical* of Siam; and the various and singular fashions of Japanese coins. The gold *cobang*, for instance, though it measures two and a half inches by one and a half, is worth only $6.50 intrinsically; it is very thin. The silver coin is interesting from its adventures. A party of Japanese were picked up by our Exploring Expedition, far out on the Pacific Ocean, where they drifted in an open boat, and were almost starved. Their gratitude prompted them to make presents of some silver coins which they had with them. Of these specimens, every one was subsequently lost in the destruction of the Peacock, except this piece, which happened to be in the pocket of an officer on board another vessel.

The last specimen which we shall notice is that of a cluster of dollars, mixed with marine shells and deposits, and cemented upon a cannon-ball. This phenomenon is from the bottom of the ocean, and its history (copied from the Bulletin of the American Philosophical Society for 1845) is as follows:—

"Early in 1815 a naval armament was fitted out in Spain, by Ferdinand VII., for the purpose of reducing the rebellious colonies in South America. The military force of this expedition amounted to ten thousand men, of whom two thousand were on board the flag-ship San Pedro. This vessel was also freighted, to a large amount, with gunpowder, cannon-balls, and specie. The fleet touched at the island of Marguerita, near the coast of Venezuela, where, with a variety of other plunder, the San Pedro took on board eight casks of spirits. Having left the island, and making for the mainland, which was within six hours' sail, the vessel was discovered to be on fire. The flame, however, was in a fair way of being extinguished, when the steward incautiously opened one of the vessels containing ardent spirits to refresh the hands. The fire, by some accident, came in contact with the rum, and instantly the flame spread so far as to become unmanageable. The ship burnt four hours, until the powder-magazine was reached by the fire, when an explosion took place, and the wreck went down, involving in its destruction the lives of four hundred men.

"The right of working the wreck having not long since been granted by the government of Venezuela to a company of gentlemen in Baltimore, designated as the 'San Pedro Company,' measures were taken to recover the specie and other valuables known to have been on board, and a vessel, with diving-bell and workmen, was sent out in February last. The wreck was found sunk in sixty feet water, and four or five miles from the mainland. It was also found that the vessel had rested on a hard bed of coral; on this (subsequently to the catastrophe) a layer of thick mud was deposited; and over this was grown another stratum of coral, which has to be pierced to arrive at the remains of the ship.

"The diving-bell (which is five feet in diameter and five feet high) is sent down three or four times a day, with two laborers, who remain down about two hours at a time. During the past season they have brought up a quantity of copper, in various shapes, besides cannon-balls, &c.; and Spanish dollars, the recoinage of which at the mint has produced about $ 18,500 [now over $ 80,000]. The silver has been much corroded by the action of *sulphur*, which is supposed to have occurred from the usual precaution of placing the specie in the powder-magazine. This has occasioned a diminution in value of 7 or 8 per cent., that is, the dollars average 92 or 93 cents each; but the *variation* of loss is very great, as some are found worth 98 cents, and one, with the stamps still visible, was reduced to 34 cents in value. They are all too much spoiled for currency, though in most cases the impressions are very distinct."

ADDITIONS.

THE following are among the most remarkable specimens added to the collection since the former publication.

1. Silver tetradrachm of Cyrenaica, Greek colony on the northeastern border of Africa; 208 grains; in very fine preservation, and of beautiful workmanship. On the obverse, head of *Jupiter Ammon.* Reverse, the *sylphion*, an umbelliferous plant of the country, the juice of which was an article of commerce, and was used by the ancients both as a condiment and a medicine. It is of the same family as the asafœtida plant. (This piece was procured of D. S. Macauley, Esq., late United States Consul at Tripoli, who procured it directly from the Arab who found it. The nearest modern port or town to the place where the coin was found is Bengazy, a town of Tripoli.)

2. Silver coin of the Caliph *Haroun Alraschid*, renowned in Arabian history and romance. This well-preserved specimen was lately presented to the mint collection by John P. Brown, Esq., Dragoman to the United States embassy at Constantinople. It bears no effigy of the Caliph, nor picture of any kind, owing to a rigid construction by the Mussulmans of the second Mosaic commandment, by which they abstain from "making the likeness of any thing," for any purpose. Instead of such emblems the coin is covered on both sides with Arabic inscriptions, chiefly texts from the Koran, with a fanciful, dashing script, peculiar to the Mahomedan coins of that day. On one side, we read in the centre, "There is no God but one God, to whom there is no Fellow." And around this, "In the name of God, this dirhem was coined in the City of Peace (Bagdad) in the year 188" that is, 803 of the Christian era.

On the reverse, the central inscription reads, "Mahomed is the messenger of God." Around this is the legend, "Mahomed is the messenger of God, whom he sent as the director of the true religion, that he might elevate it above all religions, however much the *Associators* should be displeased by it." The term *associators* was applied by Mahomed to the Christians, in respect to the doctrine of the Trinity, and probably, also, to the divine honors paid to the Virgin Mary, in the Greek Catholic Church, to which he was neighbor.

The occasion of this peculiar feature of Arabian coinage (*Cufic* coinage as it is called by numismatists) is detailed by Arabian writers, and is gathered from Marsden, in his *Numismata Orientalia.*

Until the year of the Hegira 76, or A. D. 695, the Mahomedan empire had no coinage of its own, relying upon what was already current in the country, especially of the Greek-Roman issue, from Constantinople. But the Caliph Abdalmalek having adhered to the practice of commencing his epistles to the Roman Emperor with the formulary, "There is but one God, and Mahomed is his prophet," the latter took offence at what appeared to him an insult, or at least a disparagement of the faith he professed, and threatened to retaliate by introducing inscriptions upon the coinage which would not be agreeable to the professors of Islamism. The effect of this unwise controversy was such as might have been expected. The Caliph took measures for establishing an orthodox mint of his own, and commenced a coinage in A. D. 695, the year in which the Emperor, Justinian the Second, was, for his cruelties, dethroned by his own people, with the additional indignity of having his nose and ears cut off.

It should be added, that the *denomination* of this coin (dirhem) is a change of the ancient Greek word, drachm. The average value of the Arabic dirhem was about twelve cents. The silver appears to be of a high grade of fineness.

The coin is as yet scarcely known in this country, and is very scarce even in Europe, especially in such fine preservation. Yet it is remarkable that two of such pieces have been dug up of late years in different places in *England*, where they were probably carried by returning Crusaders.

3. Silver dirhem of the Caliph *Al-Mamoun.* A. H. 203, or A. D. 818. Mahomedan legends, as on the preceding. (Also from Mr. Brown.) Well preserved.

4. Silver dirhem of *Abdallah*, Caliph of *Spain*, about A. D. 900. Mahomedan legends. In fine preservation. Struck at Cordova. (Bought at the sale of Dr. Roper's collection.)

5. Rupee of *Shah Jehan*, Mogul Emperor of Hindustan. Mahomedan symbols. This piece, in connection with the preceding, will afford an illustration of the wide diffusion of the Mahomedan faith. Date, about A. D. 1630.

6. Fifteen silver coins of France, of the Middle Ages ; commencing with Charlemagne. Well preserved.

7. Penny of Ethelbert, King of Kent, and elder brother of Alfred the Great ; died A. D. 866. (One of the pieces found in Sussex, in 1804.) In perfect preservation.

8. Rupees of Cashmere and Cabool.

9. Double-pistareen, of Philip V., Spain.

10. Hungarian coins, gold and silver, with Magyar legends, struck during the late revolution. (From the exiles.)

11. Coins of the recent republic of Venice.

12. Gold coin of Sebastian of Portugal, A. D. 1557.

13. Complete set of California gold pieces ; twenty-nine varieties.

LIST OF ENGRAVINGS,

DESCRIBED IN THE VOLUME ENTITLED

New Varieties of Gold and Silver Coins, Counterfeit Coins, and Bullion.

1.—Recent Coins of the World. 2.—Recent Counterfeit Coins. 3.—Gold from California. 4.—Recapitulation of the Net Mint Values of Gold and Silver Coins, issued within twenty-five years. 5.—Silver from Lake Superior. 6.—Table of Correspondence between Pennyweights and Grains, and the Decimal Fractions of a Troy Ounce. 7.—Comparison of American and Foreign Weights used for Precious Metals. 8.—Bulk and Packing of Precious Metals. 9.—Determination of the Value of a Specimen of Gold or Silver in its Native Rock or Gauge. 10.—Transaction of Business at the Mint.

By JACOB R. ECKFELDT *and* W. E. DU BOIS, *Assayers of the U. S. Mint.*

PLATE FIRST.

No. 1.—HALF EAGLE, 1849. N. G. and W.
" 3.—FIVE DOLLARS, Oregon Exchange Company.
" 4.—TEN DOLLARS, Miners' Bank, San Francisco.
" 5.—TEN DOLLARS, Moffatt and Company, 1849–1850.
" 6.—FIVE DOLLARS, Moffatt and Company, 1849–1850.
" 11.—FIVE DOLLARS, Pacific Company, 1849.
" 12.—FIVE DOLLARS, Massachusetts and California Company.
" 21.—FIVE DOLLARS, Shultz and Company.

PLATE SECOND.

No. 7.—TEN DOLLARS, J. S. O. (Ormsby of Pennsylvania.)
" 9.—TEN DOLLARS, Templeton Reid, Assayer.
" 10.—TEN DOLLARS, Pacific Company, 1849.
" 16.—TEN DOLLARS, Baldwin and Company, 1850.
" 17.—TEN DOLLARS, Baldwin and Company, 1851.
" 18.—FIVE DOLLARS, Baldwin and Company, 1850.
" 19.—TEN DOLLARS, Dubosq and Company, 1850.
" 25.—TWO AND A HALF DOLLARS, Mormon Coin, Utah.

PLATE THIRD.

No. 2.—TEN DOLLARS, Oregon Exchange Company.
" 13.—TEN DOLLARS, Cincinnati Mining and Trading Company, 1849.
" 14.—FIVE DOLLARS, Cincinnati Mining and Trading Company, 1849.
" 20.—FIVE DOLLARS, Dubosq and Company, 1850.
" 22.—TWENTY DOLLARS, Mormon Coin, Utah.
" 23.—TEN DOLLARS, Mormon Coin, Utah.
" 24.—FIVE DOLLARS, Mormon Coin, Utah.
" 26.—FIVE DOLLARS, Dunbar and Company.

PLATE FOURTH.

No. 8.—TWENTY-FIVE DOLLARS, Templeton Reid, Assayer, 1849.
" 15.—TWENTY DOLLARS, Baldwin and Company, 1851.
PIECE OF TEN REALS, (Silver) of New Granada.
FIFTY DOLLARS, (Gold Coin) A. Humbert, United States Assayer.

PLATE FIFTH.

No. 28.—INGOTS of Moffatt and Company, San Francisco, $16.
" 29.—INGOTS of Moffatt and Company, 10 dwt. 16 grs.
" 30.—GOLD BARS, Kohler, Assayer of California.
QUARTER DOUBLOON of Costa Rica.
QUARTER DOUBLOON of Central America.
HALF DOUBLOON of Costa Rica.
THREE CENT, (Silver Coin) United States, 1851.

☞ The whole of the above work is contained, entire, in the BANKER'S MAGAZINE for September, October, November and December, 1851.

RECENT AMERICAN COINS. PLATE FIRST.

No. 1.

No. 3.

No. 6.

No. 4.

No. 5.

No. 11.

No. 12.

No. 21.

See pp. 181, 182, 183, Bankers' Magazine, Vol. VI.,—or pp. 7, 8, 9, Work on Coins.

RECENT AMERICAN COINS. PLATE SECOND.

No. 10. No. 25. No 9.

No 16. No 7.

No. 19 No. 18. No. 17.

See pp. 181, 182, 183, Bankers' Magazine, Vol. VI.—or pp. 7, 8, 9, Work on Coins.

RECENT AMERICAN COINS. PLATE THIRD.

No. 23.

No. 20.

No. 2.

No. 13.

No. 22.

No. 26.

No. 24.

No. 14.

See pp. 181, 182, 183, Bankers' Magazine, Vol. VI.—or pp. 7, 8, 9, Work on Coins.

RECENT AMERICAN COINS. PLATE FOURTH.

Piece of Ten Reals, (silver) New Granada.

No. 8.

No. 15.

See pp. 181, 182, 183, Bankers' Magazine, Vol. VI.—or pp. 7, 8, 9, Work on Coins.

RECENT AMERICAN COINS. PLATE FIFTH.

Quarter Doubloon of Costa Rica.

Quarter Doubloon of Central America.

Half Doubloon o: Costa Rica

No 30.

F. D. KOHLER
STATE ASSAYER DWT
CARAT CAL = 44 3/4
21 1/8 1850 CTS
$40.07

Three Cent Coin.

No. 28.

No. 29.

See pp. 181, 182, 183, Bankers' Magazine, Vol. VI.—or pp. 7, 8, 9, Work on Coins.

THE

MERCHANT'S AND BANKER'S

ALMANAC

FOR

1852.

CONTAINING,

I. Calendar and Chronology of Important Events.
II. The Banks of the United States in 1851. 1. Name and Location of each. 2. Names of President and Cashier of each. 3. Capital of each.
III. Synopsis of the Usury Laws, &c., of the States. 1. Legal Rates of Interest, and Penalties for the violation thereof. 2. Damages on Inland and Foreign Bills of Exchange. 3 Grace on Sight Bills. 4. Decisions of the State Courts.
IV. Coinage, Public Debt, Revenue, Expenditures, Post-offices, and Sales of Public Lands, of the United States, for each year from 1790 to 1850.
V. Public Debt, Revenue, and Expenditure of each State in the Union.
VI. Official Value of Foreign Coins at the Sub-Treasury and Custom-House of the U. S.
VII. Fluctuations of Stocks at New York each month in 1850.
VIII. Fluctuations of Stocks at Baltimore each month in 1849.
IX. Highest and Lowest Prices of English Funds each year from 1731 to 1848.
X. Highest and Lowest Prices of English Funds each month from 1847 to 1851.
XI. Table of Loans raised for Great Britain, and rates of Interest from 1793 to 1847.
XII. Rates of Exchange between New York and London each month from 1822 to 1850.
XIII. Forms of Bills of Exchange in Eight European Languages.
XIV. Tables of English and Scotch Money, during each reign, from 1066 to 1816.
XV. Tables of the Moneys of Account of various nations.
XVI. Tables of the Assay, Weight and Value of the Gold and Silver Coins of all nations.
XVII. The Bank of England. Directors from 1694 to 1847.
XVIII. Annual Dividends and Prices of Stock of the Bank of England from 1694 to 1847.
XIX. Public Debt, Revenue and Expenditure of the U. S. for the year ending June 30, 1850.
XX. Forms of Letters of Credit as used in New York and London for India Remittances.
XXI. The Banks of England, Ireland, and Scotland enumerated, with their Circulation and Coin.
XXII. List of the London Private Bankers and Members of the Clearing-House.
XXIII. Notes on a few Coins in general use.
XXIV. Abstract of the Laws of the U. S. 1. Of the Mint. 2. Of Foreign Coins current in the U. S.
XXV. Laws of the State of New York. 1. To organize a Bank Department. 2. The Bank Note Redemption Law. 3. New Insurance Law of New York.
XXVI. Miscellaneous Information.

To be Continued Annually.

PUBLISHED BY

PHILLIPS, SAMPSON & CO., 110 WASHINGTON STREET, BOSTON:
GEORGE P. PUTNAM, 155 BROADWAY, NEW YORK:
A. HART, PHILADELPHIA.

CONTENTS.

JANUARY.

MOON'S PHASES.

FULL MOON,...... 7d. 1h. 25m. M. | NEW MOON,......21d. 2h. 43m. M.
LAST QUARTER, 13d. 8h. 34m. A. | FIRST QUARTER, 29d. 5h. 50m. M.

Day of Month.	Day of Week.	MEMORANDA.	SUN Rises. H. M.	SUN Sets. H. M.
1	Thu	1848. The State of Maryland resumed payment of interest···	7 30	4 39
2	Frid	1829. Banking Capital of New York City $18,350,000······	7 30	4 39
3	Sat	1829. Banking Capital of Boston $15,050,000··············	7 30	4 40
4	SUN	1829. Banking Capital of Philadelphia $11,290,000 ·········	7 30	4 41
5	Mon	1720. John Law appointed Comptroller-Gen. of French finances	7 30	4 42
6	Tue	1837. Country Redempt'n by Suffolk Bk., for '36, $126,000,000	7 30	4 43
7	Wed	1840. Banking Capital of Philad. $16,000,000 (ex. B. U. S.)	7 30	4 44
8	Thu	1786. Nicholas Biddle born at Philadelphia················	7 29	4 45
9	Frid	···	7 29	4 46
10	Sat	1765. Stamp Act passed by the British Parliament···········	7 29	4 47
11	SUN	1569. Drawing of the first English Lottery·················	7 29	4 48
12	Mon	···	7 28	4 49
13	Tue	1841. Pennsylvania Bank U. S. shares sold at 50············	7 28	4 50
14	Wed	1639. First Convention met in Connecticut to form constitution.	7 28	4 51
15	Thu	1841. Banks of Phila. and Wilmington resumed specie payment.	7 27	4 53
16	Frid	1707. Union of Eng. and Scotl'd ratified by Scottish parliament.	7 27	4 54
17	Sat	1776. Daniel & Robert Perreau executed at Tyburn for forgery.	7 26	4 55
18	SUN	1833. U. S. Bank Shares in London, £22 10, ($109)········	7 26	4 56
19	Mon	···	7 25	4 57
20	Tue	1733. Robert Morris, the financier, was born at Liverpool·····	7 25	4 59
21	Wed	1721. South Sea Bubble burst······························	7 24	5 0
22	Thu	···	7 23	5 1
23	Frid	1840. Sub-Treasury Act passed····························	7 23	5 2
24	Sat	1811. Bill to re-charter Bank U. S. rejected by House of Reps.	7 22	5 3
25	SUN	···	7 21	5 5
26	Mon	1850. Lord Jeffrey died at Edinburgh·····················	7 21	5 6
27	Tue	1842. The Girard Bank stopped business···················	7 20	5 7
28	Wed	1842. Capital of forty-two banks in Maine $3,514,000········	7 19	5 8
29	Thu	1761. Albert Gallatin born at Geneva, Switzerland··········	7 18	5 10
30	Frid	1815. Veto of the U. S. Bank Bill, by President Madison····	7 17	5 11
31	Sat	1823. The Exchange Bank at Salem, chartered··············	7 16	5 13

Foreign Exchanges.—An adverse state of foreign exchanges, from whatever cause arising, and whether temporary or otherwise, is to be corrected by making money scarce, and thereby lowering the value of all merchandise, until by the depreciation a market is forced for it abroad. Do these reasoners comprehend the losses occasioned by this depreciation of all property when this screw is applied to correct every occasional fluctuation of the exchanges? And, moreover, how uselessly these sacrifices are increased in cases like the present, when the difficulty to be guarded against is not real, but the result of a fanciful scale of paper and bullion which imagines dangers, while there is a larger portion of treasure in the bank than the average of many years of supposed abundance. If our trade is to be so governed, and liable to these caprices, is it too much to say, that the advantages of a paper circulation are overbalanced by its inconveniencies and dangers?—*Lord Ashburton.*

FEBRUARY.

MOON'S PHASES.

FULL MOON,....... 5d. 2h. 9m. A.	NEW MOON,...... 19d. 8h. 10m. A.
LAST QUARTER, 12d. 5h. 18m. M.	FIRST QUARTER, 28d. 0h. 47m. M.

Day of Month.	Day of Week.	MEMORANDA.	SUN Rises. H. M.	SUN Sets. H. M.
1	SUN	1835. Banking Capital of Boston, $18,150,000	7 15	5 14
2	Mon	1831. America, Phenix, Mech., & Merch. Bks., N.Y., chartered.	7 14	5 15
3	Tue	1840. Total Banking Capital of Pennsylvania, $59,000,000	7 13	5 16
4	Wed	1839. The Union Bank, London, commenced business	7 11	5 18
5	Thu	1841. Bank U. S., of Pa., suspended payment	7 10	5 19
6	Frid	1837. Coin in Bank of England reduced to £4,032,000	7 9	5 20
7	Sat	1784. The Massachusetts Bank in Boston, chartered	7 8	5 21
8	SUN	1838. Coin in Bank of England, £10,471,000	7 7	5 23
9	Mon	1773. General William Henry Harrison born, in Virginia	7 6	5 24
10	Tue	1841. Philadelphia and Baltimore bank notes 5 per cent. disc't.	7 4	5 25
11	Wed	1828. De Witt Clinton died aged 59	7 3	5 27
12	Thu	1819. The Commercial Bank, Salem, Massachusetts, chartered	7 2	5 28
13	Frid	1816. Bank circulation in Kentucky $1,308,000	7 0	5 29
14	Sat	1817. Specie held by all the Pennsylvania Banks $1,930,000	6 58	5 31
15	SUN	1822. William Pinckney died at Washington, aged 58	6 58	5 32
16	Mon	1826. Lindley Murray died, aged 81	6 56	5 33
17	Tue	1841. Chitty, the writer on bills and notes, died, aged 66	9 55	5 34
18	Wed	1791. Vermont admitted into the Union	6 54	5 36
19	Thu	....	6 52	5 37
20	Frid	1793. Failure of Lane, Son & Fraser, bankers, London	6 51	5 38
21	Sat	1848. John Quincy Adams died at Washington, aged 81.	6 49	5 39
22	SUN	1732. George Washington born, at Bridge's Creek, Virginia	6 48	5 41
23	Mon	1846. Battle of Buena Vista, (22d and 23d)	6 46	5 42
24	Tue	1772. W. H. Crawford, b. Nelson Co., V., 1822, Coutts, the bkr. d.	6 45	5 43
25	Wed	1820. William Ellery died, aged 93	6 43	5 44
26	Thu	1797. Order in Council to suspend specie pay't by Bk. of Eng	6 42	5 46
27	Frid	1844. Nicholas Riddle died near Philadelphia, aged 58	6 40	5 47
28	Sat	1826. Coin in Bank of England reduced to £2,460,000	6 38	5 48
29	SUN	....	6 37	5 49

Public Credit.—The huge accumulations of capital in the hands of individuals; their necessity of obtaining a profitable return for it; the industry, enterprise, intelligence and commercial spirit of other large portions of the community not possessed of sufficient capital of their own, in order to give full exercise for their powers, bring these two classes together in the characters of creditors and debtors, of lenders and borrowers, by an impulse too strong and certain to be controlled. They are brought together in various forms: some in the simple shape of the capitalist lending, and the active merchant or manufacturer borrowing; some in the shape of sleeping partnerships; some in the shape of large wholesale dealers; who employ large capitals in furnishing credit to smaller dealers, who distribute commodities to the consumers.—*London Economist.*

MARCH.

MOON'S PHASES.

FULL MOON,...... 6d. 0h. 46m. M.	NEW MOON,.......20d. 1h. 58m. A.
LAST QUARTER, 12d. 3h. 45m. A.	FIRST QUARTER, 28d. 4h. 5m. A.

Day of Month.	Day of Week.	MEMORANDA.	SUN Rises. H.	M.	Sets. H.	M.
1	Mon	1833. Banking Capital of Philadelphia, paid in, $18,935,000··	6	35	5	51
2	Tue	1833. 600 shares Bank U. S. Stock sold in New York at 105.·	6	34	5	52
3	Wed	1836. Charter of the Bank U. S. expired by limitation······	6	32	5	53
4	Thu	1822. Funeral of Coutts, the banker ······················	6	30	5	54
5	Frid	1833. Bills issued in German by the Western Bank, Philad···	6	28	5	55
6	Sat	··	6	27	5	57
7	SUN	1848. French Five per cents 97½ (22 February, 116,)········	6	25	5	58
8	Mon	1803. The Salem Bank, Salem, Massachusetts, chartered·····	6	24	5	59
9	Tue	1835. Bank U. S. shares sold at 108························	6	22	6	0
10	Wed	1834. The London and Westminster Bank commenced business.	6	20	6	1
11	Thu	1797. Bank of England notes for £1 and £2 first issued······	6	18	6	2
12	Frid	1837. Banking Capital of Baltimore City, $8,611,000········	6	17	6	4
13	Sat	1837. The *Mont De Piété*, at Limerick established··········	6	15	6	5
14	SUN	··	6	13	6	6
15	Mon	1848. Edict for suspension of specie payments by Bk. of France,	6	12	6	7
16	Tue	1680. First General Assembly held in New Hampshire.······	6	10	6	8
17	Wed	1787. Bank of North America re-incorporated by Congress···	6	8	6	9
18	Thu	1782. John C. Calhoun born, Abbeville District, S. C.·······	6	6	6	10
19	Frid	1814. Gov. Snyder's Veto Message of the Penn. Bank bills···	6	5	6	12
20	Sat	1831. The City Bank, New York, robbed of $245,000·······	6	3	6	13
21	SUN	1729. John Law, projector of Miss. Scheme, d. at Venice, a. 58.	6	1	6	14
22	Mon	1833. U. S. Governm't bill on France protested for F. 4,856,666	5	59	6	15
23	Tue	··	5	58	6	16
24	Wed	1834. The Bk. of Maryland, at Baltimore, failed for $1,600,000.	5	56	6	17
25	Thu	1698. The Bk. of England authorized to pay semiannual div.	5	54	6	18
26	Frid	··	5	52	6	19
27	Sat	··	5	51	6	20
28	SUN	1834. Senate U. S. disapproved removal of Deposits, 26 to 20.	5	49	6	22
29	Mon	1836. Bank U. S. chartered by Pensylvania.—'48. Astor died.	5	47	6	23
30	Tue	··	5	45	6	24
31	Wed	1848. Loan of $18,000,000 authorized by Congress··········	5	44	6	25

Letter to a Student.—If your spirit be as stout and pure, as your letter indicates, you require little advice, beyond that which you will find within the walls of your university. A brave and pure spirit is worth more than "half the battle," not only in preparing for life, but in all its conflicts. Take it for granted, that there is no excellence without great labor. No mere aspirations for eminence, however ardent, will do the business. Wishing, and sighing, and imagining, and dreaming of greatness, will never make you great. If you would get to the mountain top upon which the temple of fame stands, it will not do to stand still, looking, admiring, and wishing you were there. You must gird up your loins and go to work with all the indomitable energy of Hannibal scaling the Alps.—*Wirt.*

APRIL.

MOON'S PHASES.

FULL MOON, ...4d. 9h. 39m. M. | NEW MOON, ... 19d. 7h. 1m. M.
LAST QUARTER, 11d. 4h. 15m. M. | FIRST QUARTER, 27d. 3h. 19m. M.

Day of Month.	Day of Week.	MEMORANDA.	SUN Rises. H.	M.	Sets. H.	M.
1	Thu	1828. Banking Capital of Vermont, $321,000	5	42	6	26
2	Frid	1799. Manhattan Bk. chart. granted by State of N. Y., *unlimited*	5	40	6	27
3	Sat	1837. Fifty-five Banks in Maine; capital $5,074,000	5	39	6	28
4	SUN	1835. Banking Capital of Rhode Island $8,750,000	5	37	6	30
5	Mon	1842. Lord Ashburton arrived at Washington, via Annapolis.	5	35	6	31
6	Tue	1789. George Washington elected first President of the U. S.	5	33	6	32
7	Wed	1841. United States Treasury notes outstanding $6,300,000 ...	5	32	6	33
8	Thu	....	5	30	6	34
9	Frid	1842. New York State Five per cents sold at 78	5	28	6	35
10	Sat	1792. Bank of Albany incorporated	5	27	6	36
11	SUN	1848. French Five per cents fell to 51, (116 Feb. 22).	5	25	6	37
12	Mon	1777. Henry Clay born	5	23	6	38
13	Tue	1840. Bank of Virginia lost $540,000 by teller	5	22	6	40
14	Wed	1825. Charter (*unlimited.*) granted to N. Y. Dry Dock Bank.	5	20	6	41
15	Thu	1842. Pennsylvania Five per cents sold at 39	5	19	6	42
16	Frid	1838. Bank Convention at N. Y. fixed 10th May for resumption.	5	17	6	43
17	Sat	1830. Greenwich Bank, N. Y., chartered till June 1, 1855	5	15	6	44
18	SUN	1842. Ohio Six per cents sold at 61	5	14	6	45
19	Mon	1772. David Ricardo, the banker and broker, born	5	12	6	46
20	Tue	1833. Seventh Ward Bank, N. Y., chartered till Jan. 1, 1863.	5	11	6	47
21	Wed	1842. Indiana Five per cents sold at 19.	5	9	6	48
22	Thu	....	5	8	6	50
23	Frid	1832. Leather Manufacturers' Bk., N. Y., chart'd till June 1, '62.	5	6	6	51
24	Sat	....	5	5	6	52
25	SUN	....	5	3	6	53
26	Mon	1841. Sales of Pennsylvania Bank U. S. shares at $17\frac{1}{2}$.	5	2	6	54
27	Tue	1848. Edict to incorporate Bk. of France with nine Branches.	5	0	6	55
28	Wed	....	4	59	6	56
29	Thu	1829. Ontario Bk., Canandaigua, and Branch chartered till 1857	4	58	6	58
30	Frid	1829. The National Bank, N. Y., chartered till Jan. 1, 1857 ...	4	56	6	59

Public Credit.—But Public Credit and Public Order are essentially bound up with each other, and with the maintenance of general prosperity. An infringement of either or both is the first and surest signal of derangement in commerce, and lessened employment. At the present moment, when the state of Europe furnishes so many sad examples of the misery and ruin which have resulted to the commercial and working classes, it is of the greatest importance that we should form a just estimate of the consequences which would result in this country to the various classes of society, from any important interruption to that peace and order for which it has been generally so much distinguished, and under which, in comparison with those countries which have been exposed to continual outbreaks, it has risen to so much social and general prosperity.—*London Economist.*

MAY.

MOON'S PHASES.

FULL MOON,...... 3d. 5h. 38m. A. | NEW MOON,...... 18d. 10h. 31m. A.
LAST QUARTER, 10d. 6h. 39m. A. | FIRST QUARTER, 26d. 10h. 54m. M.

Day of Month	Day of Week.	MEMORANDA.	SUN Rises. H.	M.	Sets. H.	M.
1	Sat	1821. The Bank of England resumed specie payments.	4	55	6	59
2	SUN	1769. The Duke of Wellington born.	4	53	7	1
3	Mon	1797. Bank Restriction Act passed by Parliament.	4	52	7	2
4	Tue	1819. City Bank, Baltimore, failed — Cashier resigned.	4	51	7	3
5	Wed	1821. Napoleon Bonaparte died, aged 52.	4	49	7	4
6	Thu	1695. Bank of England loan money on plate, tin, copper, &c.	4	48	7	5
7	Frid	1835. Books of subscription to Merchants' Bank, Balt., opened.	4	47	7	6
8	Sat	1806. Robt. Morris died at Philadelphia, aged 73.	4	46	7	7
9	SUN	1846. Battle of Palo Alto, (8th and 9th.)	4	45	7	8
10	Mon	1837. Suspension of payt's by N. Y. City Banks. '38. Resumed.	4	43	7	9
11	Tue	...	4	42	7	10
12	Wed	1846. War declared against Mexico by Congress.	4	41	7	12
13	Thu	1833. Demand by Bk. U. S. *on Treas.* for damgs. on French bill.	4	40	7	13
14	Frid	1817. Scrip Stock B. U. S. sold at $100, for $65 paid.	4	39	7	14
15	Sat	1783. Charter granted to the Bank of Ireland, cap. £600,000.	4	38	7	15
16	SUN	...	4	37	7	16
17	Mon	1849. Great Fire in St. Louis.	4	36	7	17
18	Tue	1836. Bank of the State of New York chartered till Jan. 1, 1866.	4	35	7	18
19	Wed	1647. First General Assembly of R. Island met at Portsmouth.	4	34	7	19
20	Thu	1716 Patent granted for Law's Bank in France.	4	33	7	20
21	Frid	1835. Spanish stock fell in the London Market 16 per cent.	4	32	7	21
22	Sat	1807. Aaron Burr's trial commenced at Richmond.	4	32	7	22
23	SUN	1609. Second Charter granted to Virginia by King James.	4	31	7	23
24	Mon	1750. Stephen Girard born near Bordeaux.	4	30	7	24
25	Tue	1835. Sub-Books to Merchants' Bank, Baltimore, closed.	4	29	7	24
26	Wed	1780. Charter of the first Bk. of N. Am. approved by Congress.	4	28	7	25
27	Thu	...	4	28	7	26
28	Frid	1841. Exchange at New York on Baltimore, $4\frac{1}{4}$ discount.	4	28	7	27
29	Sat	1720. Law resigned his office of Comptroller-General.	4	27	7	28
30	SUN	1848. Treaty of Peace with Mexico signed.	4	26	7	29
31	Mon	...	4	26	7	30

Paper Currency.—We thus see that in maintaining a gold currency, the country absolutely loses not only the whole interest of so much capital, but also a sum equal to the wear and tear of the coin. Any means, therefore, by which the currency can be economized, by which the same facilities can be with equal certainty and safety performed without the use of coin, offers the means of absolutely adding to the available and productive capital of the country. Without the adoption of such economical facilities, the wealth of a country would be enormously retarded. Bills of exchange, when used to pass goods from hand to hand, and the use of checks upon bankers, by which the command over money is transferred from one to another, are the chief and most extensive means used by merchants themselves to economize the use of money.—*London Economist.*

JUNE.

MOON'S PHASES.

FULL MOON,......2d. 1h. 41m. M. | NEW MOON, ... 17d. 0h. 3m. A.
LAST QUARTER, 9d. 10h. 31m. M. | FIRST QUARTER, 24d. 4h. 3m. A.

Day of Month.	Day of Week.	MEMORANDA.	SUN Rises. H.	M.	SUN Sets. H.	M.
1	Tue	1837. Three American Bankers in London failed............	4	25	7	30
2	Wed	1720. South Sea Stock sold at 890 per 100 paid in..........	4	25	7	31
3	Thu	1801. Corner Stone laid of the new Bank of Scotland.......	4	25	7	32
4	Frid	1834. Specie held by the Bank of the U. S. $12,298,000.....	4	24	7	32
5	Sat	1734. Bank of England commenced business, Threadneedle St.	4	24	7	33
6	SUN	1835. Maryland Loan of $2,000,000 taken at 16 premium....	4	23	7	34
7	Mon	1832. Celebrated Reform Bill, in Great Britain passed.......	4	23	7	34
8	Tue	1845. Andrew Jackson died, aged 78......................	4	23	7	35
9	Wed	1784. The Bank of N. York (first bank,) commenced business.	4	23	7	35
10	Thu	....	4	22	7	36
11	Frid	1832. U. S. Bank bill passed by Senate U. S., 28 to 20.......	4	22	7	36
12	Sat	1824. The Asiatic Bank, at Salem, chartered.............	4	22	7	37
13	SUN	1812. Circulation of all the banks in Rhode Island $460,000..	4	22	7	37
14	Mon	1850. Destructive Fire in San Francisco—loss $5,000,000....	4	22	7	38
15	Tue	....	4	22	7	38
16	Wed	....	4	22	7	38
17	Thu	1775. Battle of Bunker Hill..........................	4	22	7	39
18	Frid	1799. The Essex Bank, at Salem, chartered................	4	23	7	39
19	Sat	1812. War declared against Great Britain.................	4	23	7	40
20	SUN	1830. Branch Bank U. S., Boston, robbed of $40,000 by teller.	4	23	7	40
21	Mon	....	4	23	7	40
22	Tue	1812. Federal Republican Riot in Baltimore..............	4	23	7	40
23	Wed	1697. Bank of England notes 13 to 14 per cent. discount.....	4	24	7	40
24	Thu	1819. Bank United States shares sold at 89 to 90...........	4	24	7	40
25	Frid	1783. The Bank of Ireland commenced business...........	4	24	7	40
26	Sat	1811. The Merchants' Bank, at Salem, chartered...........	4	25	7	40
27	SUN	1777. Rev. Dr. Dodd exctd. for forging name of Lord Chesterf'ld	4	25	7	40
28	Mon	1836. James Madison died, aged 85......................	4	25	7	40
29	Tue	....	4	26	7	40
30	Wed	1841. First Annual Meeting of the Commercial Bk. of London.	4	26	7	40

Literary Pursuits of Merchants.—Biography abounds in truth, with examples of the union of the pursuits of literature and science with those of every department of active life. The most elegant of the writers of ancient Rome, was also the most renowned of her warriors. It was amid the hurry and toils of his campaigns that Julius Cæsar is said to have written those commentaries, or memoirs of his military exploits, which have immortalized his name more than all his victories, and thus amply justified the anxiety he is recorded to have shown to preserve the work, when, being obliged to throw himself from his ship, in the bay of Alexandria, and swim for his life, he made his way to the shore, with his arms in one hand, holding his commentaries with his teeth.—*Brougham.*

JULY.

MOON'S PHASES.

FULL MOON,...... 1d. 10h. 43m. M. | NEW MOON,..... 16d. 11h. 31m. A.
LAST QUARTER, 9d. 5h. 22m. M. | FIRST QUARTER, 23d. 8h. 17m. A.
FULL MOON, 30d. 9h. 27m. A.

Day of Month.	Day of Week.	MEMORANDA.	SUN Rises. H.	M.	Sets. H.	M.
1	Thu	1845. Cheap Postage Bill went into operation.	4	27	7	40
2	Frid	1800. Union of Great Britain with Ireland by act of Parliament.	4	27	7	40
3	Sat	1832. Charter of U. S. Bank passed by House Reps.,1 07 to 85	4	28	7	40
4	SUN	1840. Sub-Treasury Bill approved by President Van Buren.	4	28	7	40
5	Mon	1766. Jacob Perkins, celebrated bank note engraver, born	4	29	7	39
6	Tue	1837. Total banking capital of New York State, $34,000,000	4	29	7	39
7	Wed	1850. President Taylor died at Washington, aged 66	4	30	7	39
8	Thu	1840. First Annual meeting of the Union Bank of London	4	31	7	38
9	Frid	1847. Richard Biddle died in Pittsburg	4	32	7	38
10	Sat	1832. Veto of Bank U. S. charter, by President Jackson	4	33	7	37
11	SUN	1848. Canal Bank, Albany, failed	4	33	7	37
12	Mon		4	34	7	36
13	Tue		4	35	7	36
14	Wed		4	36	7	35
15	Thu		4	36	7	34
16	Frid		4	37	7	34
17	Sat	1792. Discounts first granted by Bank of Albany	4	38	7	33
18	SUN	1840. Cunard Steamer Britannia arrived at Boston	4	39	7	32
19	Mon		4	40	7	32
20	Tue		4	41	7	31
21	Wed		4	42	7	30
22	Thu	1835. Northern Bank of Ky., Lexington, commenced business	4	43	7	29
23	Frid	1838. Bank Convention held at Philadelphia	4	44	7	28
24	Sat	1846. Preserved Fish, President Tradesman's Bk , N. Y., died.	4	44	7	28
25	SUN		4	45	7	27
26	Mon		4	46	7	26
27	Tue	1694. Charter granted to Bank of England, cap. £1,200,000	4	47	7	25
28	Wed	1836. Nathan M. Rothschild, London, d., Frankfort O. M., a. 60.	4	48	7	23
29	Thu	1830. Charles X dethroned in France.	4	49	7	22
30	Frid	1849. Jacob Perkins, inventor of steel plates, d. in London, a. 83.	4	50	7	21
31	Sat		4	51	7	20

Origin of Repudiation.—In proportion precisely as an individual is beyond the reach of compulsory process, should he be inclined to disregard the technicalities of mere law, and base himself upon the broader principles of natural justice. This is still more necessary when an independent sovereignty is concerned, because it is more difficult to procure redress for wrongs committed by a State. The relation between debtor and creditor in all cases involving the repose of confidence, is pre-eminently a fiduciary relation when the debtor is a sovereign commonwealth. It should be distinguished by that *uberrima fides* which scorns the strict letter of the contract and regards its spirit and intention.—*Peleg W. Chandler.*

AUGUST.

MOON'S PHASES.

LAST QUARTER, 7d. 8h. 22m. A. | FIRST QUARTER, 22d. 1h. 17m. M.
NEW MOON,......15d. 9h. 13m. M. | FULL MOON,......29d. 10h. 22m. M.

Day of Month.	Day of Week.	MEMORANDA.	SUN Rises. H. M.	SUN Sets. H. M.
1	SUN	1838. Specie payment resumed by Bank State N. C·········	4 52	7 19
2	Mon	1843. 103 Banks in Massachusetts, capital $31,000,000·······	4 53	7 18
3	Tue	1732. Corner Stone laid of Bank of England, Threadneedle st.	4 54	7 17
4	Wed	1837. Sales of U. S. Bank stock, 118¾··················	4 55	7 15
5	Thu	1829. Wm. F. Saul, cash'r Bk. Orleans, N. O., com't'd suicide.	4 57	7 14
6	Frid	1846. Sub-Treasury Bill passed by Congress···············	4 58	7 13
7	Sat	1842. Exchange at New York on London, 6¾ premium·······	4 59	7 12
8	SUN	1835. Bk. of Md. riots in Balt. 1836. Fun'l of N. M. Rothschild.	5 0	7 10
9	Mon	1841. Sub-Treasury act repealed,······················	5 1	7 9
10	Tue	··	5 2	7 8
11	Wed	1842. New York City seven per cent. loan negotiated at par··	5 3	7 6
12	Thu	1849. Albert Gallatin died at Astoria, L. I., aged 89········	5 4	7 5
13	Frid	1720. Scire Facias issued against the South Sea Company····	5 5	7 3
14	Sat	1838. Resumption of specie payments in Penn., Ohio and Ky.·	5 6	7 2
15	SUN	1837. Convention held of the New York City Banks·········	5 7	7 0
16	Mon	1841. Veto of the Fiscal Bank U. S., by President Tyler····	5 8	6 59
17	Tue	1841. Repeal of the Sub-Treasury act signed by Pres. Tyler··	5 9	6 57
18	Wed	1841. Gen. b'kr'p'cy law passed Cong. '38. Sale $5,000,000 bds.	5 10	6 56
19	Thu	1843. Circ'lat'n of b'ks in Mass. $9,200,000. [Union Bk., Miss.	5 11	6 54
20	Frid	1847. Battle of Churubusco···························	5 13	6 53
21	Sat	1841. Danville Branch Farmers' Bank, Va., robbed of $92,000	5 14	6 51
22	SUN	1842. The Ashburton Treaty ratified by the Senate········	5 15	6 50
23	Mon	··	5 16	6 48
24	Tue	1814. Public Buildings at Washington burnt by the British···	5 17	6 47
25	Wed	1789. The Mother of Washington died···················	5 18	6 45
26	Thu	1850. Louis Philippe died, aged 77······················	5 19	6 43
27	Frid	1841. Pennsylvania Bank, U. S. shares sold at 9 per cent·····	5 20	6 42
28	Sat	1843. Coin held by the Banks in Boston $6,500,000·········	5 21	6 40
29	SUN	1843. Coin held by Massachusetts Country Banks $600,000···	5 22	6 39
30	Mon	··	5 23	6 37
31	Tue	··	5 24	6 35

Utility of Banks.—The establishment of Banks, has contributed in no ordinary degree, to give security and facility to all sorts of commercial transactions. They afford safe and convenient places of deposit for the money that would otherwise have to be kept, at a considerable risk, in private houses. They also prevent, in a great measure, the necessity of carrying money from place to place to make payments, and enable them to be made in the most convenient and least expensive manner.—*J. R. McCulloch.*

SEPTEMBER.

MOON'S PHASES.

LAST QUARTER, 6d. 1h. 50m. A.	FIRST QUARTER, 20d. 8h. 33m. M.
NEW MOON,.....13d. 5h. 54m. A.	FULL MOON,......28d. 1h. 41m. M.

Day of Month.	Day of Week.	MEMORANDA.	SUN Rises. H.	M.	Sets. H.	M.
1	Wed	1835. Banking Capital of Mississippi, $12,000,000.	5	25	6	33
2	Thu	1843. Ohio State Six per cents sold at 78.	5	26	6	32
3	Frid	1844. Issue and Banking departments of Bk. of Eng. separated.	5	27	6	30
4	Sat	1841. Special assignment by Pennsylvania Bank U. S.	5	28	6	28
5	SUN	1843. Indiana State Five per cents sold at 28.	5	29	6	27
6	Mon	1843. Maryland State Six per cents sterling sold at 50.	5	30	6	25
7	Tue	1803. New York State Bank, Albany, commenced business.	5	32	6	23
8	Wed	1843. Pennsylvania State Five per cents sold at 48.	5	33	6	22
9	Thu	1841. Veto of the U. S. Fiscal Corporation bill by Pres. Tyler.	5	34	6	20
10	Frid	1608. Capt. John Smith made first President of Virginia.	5	35	6	18
11	Sat	1823. David Ricardo, banker and writer, died, aged 52.	5	36	6	16
12	SUN	1835. Merchants' Bank, of Baltimore, organized.	5	37	6	14
13	Mon	1785. Charter of the Bank of North America repealed by Penn.	5	38	6	13
14	Tue	1836. Aaron Burr died, aged 80.	5	39	6	11
15	Wed	1834. William H. Crawford died, in Georgia.	5	40	6	9
16	Thu	1843. Louisiana Five per cents (Barings's,) sold at 57.	5	41	6	7
17	Frid	1787. Constitution of the United States adopted.	5	42	6	6
18	Sat	1832. President Jackson's Manifesto read to the Cabinet.	5	43	6	4
19	SUN	1843. Virginia State Six per cents sold at 85.	5	44	6	2
20	Mon	1843. New York City Five per cents sold at 88.	5	45	6	0
21	Tue	1846. Battle of Monterey, (21st, 22d, and 23d.)	5	46	5	59
22	Wed	1843. Baltimore and Ohio Railroad shares 40.	5	47	5	57
23	Thu	1833. W. J. Duane, Sec. of Treas., removed by Pres. Jackson.	5	49	5	55
24	Frid	1813. Md. Banks nom. cap. $11,000,000, paid in $7,000,000.	5	50	5	53
25	Sat	1813. Banking Capital of Rhode Island, $1,895,000.	5	51	5	52
26	SUN	1813. Banking Capital of New York State, $21,660,000.	5	52	5	50
27	Mon	1813. Banking Capital of District of Columbia, $3,171,000.	5	53	5	48
28	Tue	1813. Circulation of District of Columbia, $1,890,000.	5	54	5	46
29	Wed	......	5	55	5	45
30	Thu	1784. Robert Morris, Superintendent Finances U. S., resigned.	5	56	5	43

A National Bank.—In making the proposition for the establishment of a national Bank, I cannot be insensible to the high authority of the names which have appeared in opposition to that measure upon constitutional grounds. It would be presumptuous to conjecture that the sentiments which actuated the opposition have passed away, and yet it would be denying to experience a great practical advantage, were we to suppose that a difference of times and circumstances would not produce a corresponding difference, in the opinions of the wisest as well as of the purest men. But in the present case a change of private opinion is not material to the success of the proposition for establishing a national Bank. In the administration of human affairs, there must be a period, when discussion shall cease, and decision shall become absolute.—*A. J. Dallas.*

OCTOBER.

MOON'S PHASES.

LAST QUARTER, 6d. 5h. 52m. M. | FIRST QUARTER, 19d. 7h. 12m. A.
NEW MOON, ... 13d. 2h. 30m. M. | FULL MOON,......27d. 7h. 10m. A.

Day of Month.	Day of Week.	MEMORANDA.	SUN Rises. H.	M.	Sets. H.	M.
1	Frid	1833. Order issued for removal of govm. Deposits from Bk. U.S.	5	57	5	41
2	Sat	1838. Resumption of specie payments in Georgia	5	58	5	39
3	SUN	....	6	0	5	38
4	Mon	1609. Henry Hudson sailed from New York for Europe	6	1	5	36
5	Tue	....	6	2	5	34
6	Wed	1773. Louis Philippe born	6	3	5	33
7	Thu	....	6	4	5	31
8	Frid	1635. John Winthrop, first Governor of Connecticut, arrived.	6	5	5	29
9	Sat	1839. The Philadelphia Banks suspended specie payments again	6	6	5	27
10	SUN	1839. The Baltimore Banks suspended specie payments	6	8	5	26
11	Mon	1791. The first Bank in Rhode Island established	6	9	5	24
12	Tue	1839. The Banks at Richmond, Va., suspended specie payments	6	10	5	23
13	Wed	1839. Bullion in Bank of England reduced to £2,300,000	6	11	5	21
14	Thu	1842. Croton Water celebration in New York	6	12	5	19
15	Frid	....	6	14	5	18
16	Sat	....	6	15	5	16
17	SUN	1735. John Adams born at Quincy	6	16	5	15
18	Mon	1827. The last British Lottery drawn	6	17	5	13
19	Tue	1630. First General Court held in Massachusetts, at Boston ...	6	18	5	11
20	Wed	1807. Aaron Burr's trial terminated at Richmond	6	19	5	10
21	Thu	1836. The London Joint Stock Bank commenced business	6	20	5	8
22	Frid	1839. Exchange on Philadelphia, at N. Y., 9 per cent. discount.	6	22	5	7
23	Sat	1667. The Royal Exchange, London, founded	6	23	5	5
24	SUN	1839. Exchange Bank of Virginia suspended.	6	24	5	4
25	Mon	1847. Bank of Eng. advanced the rate of interest to 8 per cent.	6	25	5	3
26	Tue	....	6	26	5	1
27	Wed	1827. Bank of Virginia, Petersburg, robbed of $40,000	6	28	5	0
28	Thu	1848. Harrison Gray Otis died, aged 83	6	29	4	58
29	Frid	....	6	30	4	57
30	Sat	....	6	31	4	56
31	SUN	1848. General S. W. Kearney died, aged 54	6	33	4	54

Public Credit.—Credit, public and private, is of the greatest consequence to every country; of this, it might be emphatically called the invigorating principle. No well informed man can cast a retrospective eye over the progress of the United States, from their infancy to the present period, without being convinced that they owe, in a great degree, to the fostering influence of credit, their present mature growth. This credit has been of a mixed nature, mercantile and public, foreign and domestic. Credit abroad was the trunk of our mercantile credit, from which issued ramifications that nourished all the parts of domestic labor and industry. The bills of credit emitted from time to time by the different local governments, which passed current as money, coöperated with that resource.—*Alexander Hamilton.*

NOVEMBER.

MOON'S PHASES.

LAST QUARTER, 4d. 7h. 56m. A.	FIRST QUARTER, 18d. 9h. 43m. M.
NEW MOON, ... 11d. 11h. 56m. M.	FULL MOON, ... 26d. 1h. 57m. A.

Day of Month.	Day of Week.	MEMORANDA.	SUN Rises. H. M.	SUN Sets. H. M.
1	Mon	1816. Subscriptions opened for Bank of Valley & N. W. B., Va.	6 34	4 53
2	Tue	1795. James K. Polk born in Mecklenburg Co., N. C. ·······	6 35	4 52
3	Wed	1835. Banking Capital of New Orleans, $28,000,000·······	6 36	4 51
4	Thu	···························	6 38	4 49
5	Frid	1816. Gouverneur Morris died, aged 64···················	6 39	4 48
6	Sat	1835. U. S. Branch Bk., St. Louis, sold to State Bk. of Illinois.	6 40	4 47
7	SUN	···························	6 41	4 46
8	Mon	···························	6 43	4 45
9	Tue	1848. Blum, the Leipsic bookseller, executed for treason.	6 44	4 44
10	Wed	···························	6 45	4 43
11	Thu	···························	6 46	4 42
12	Frid	···························	6 48	4 41
13	Sat	1840. U. S. Bank Shares (Penn.) sold at 68½··············	6 49	4 40
14	SUN	1827. Thomas Addis Emmet died························	6 50	4 39
15	Mon	1793. Law passed in France against Lotteries·············	6 52	4 38
16	Tue	1773. Tea destroyed in Boston Harbor····················	6 53	4 37
17	Wed	1836. Coin in Bank of England reduced to £4,933,000······	6 54	4 36
18	Thu	1816. Circulation of the Bank of Virginia $2,720,000 ·······	6 55	4 35
19	Frid	···························	6 56	4 35
20	Sat	1818. The Bank of Kentucky suspended payment··········	6 58	4 34
21	SUN	1836. London Joint Stock Bank commenced business········	6 59	4 33
22	Mon	1822. William Lowndes, of South Carolina, died············	7 0	4 33
23	Tue	1816. Circulation of the Farmers' Bank of Va., $3,310,000···	7 1	4 32
24	Wed	1844. Robbery of Rogers & Co., London Bankers, £48,000 ··	7 2	4 32
25	Thu	1829. Washington Monument, Baltimore, completed ········	7 4	4 31
26	Frid	···························	7 5	4 31
27	Sat	1837. General Convention of banks of 19 States held in N.Y.	7 6	4 30
28	SUN	···························	7 7	4 30
29	Mon	1817. Bank Capital of Maryland, paid in, $8,206,000········	7 8	4 29
30	Tue	1824. Henry Fauntleroy, a London banker, hung for forgery··	7 9	4 29

Mr. Jefferson on National Debts.—"It is a wise rule, and should be fundamental in a government disposed to cherish its credit, and at the same time to restrain the use of it within the limits of its faculties, never to borrow a dollar without laying a tax in the same instant, for paying the interest annually and the principal within a given term; and to consider that tax as pledged to the creditors on the public faith. On such a pledge as this, sacredly observed, a government may always command on a reasonable interest, all the lendable money of its citizens; whilst the necessity of an equivalent tax is a salutary warning to them and their constituents against oppression, bankruptcy, and its inevitable consequence, revolution."

DECEMBER.

MOON'S PHASES.

LAST QUARTER, 4d. 7h. 38m. M. | FIRST QUARTER, 18d. 3h. 55m. M.
NEW MOON, ... 10d. 10h. 47m. A. | FULL MOON, ... 26d. 8h. 26m. M.

Day of Month.	Day of Week.	MEMORANDA.	SUN Rises. H.	M.	Sets. H.	M.
1	Wed	....	7	10	4	29
2	Thu	1836. U. S. Bank, Philadelphia, discounted $900,000 this day.	7	11	4	28
3	Frid	1814. Treaty of Peace signed at Ghent..................	7	12	4	28
4	Sat N	1814. Specie held by the banks of Massachusetts $6,393,000..	7	13	4	28
5	SU	1796. Loyalty Loan of £18,000,000 raised in London.......	7	14	4	28
6	Mon	1841. Bank of Louisiana resumed specie payments..........	7	15	4	28
7	Tue	1828. Specie held by the Boston Banks $712,000...........	7	16	4	28
8	Wed	1848. First deposit of California gold dust at U. S. mint.....	7	17	4	28
9	Thu	1818. Loans of U. S. Bank in Baltimore, $8,400,000.........	7	18	4	28
10	Frid	1814. Total Bank capital of Massachusetts $11,140,000......	7	19	4	28
11	Sat	....	7	20	4	28
12	SUN	1825. Sir Peter Pole & Co., bankers, London, failed.........	7	20	4	28
13	Mon	1790. Hamilton's plan of National Bank submitted to Congress.	7	21	4	28
14	Tue	1799. George Washington died, aged 68..................	7	22	4	29
15	Wed	....	7	23	4	29
16	Thu	1835. Great Fire in New York—Exchange burnt...........	7	23	4	29
17	Frid	1825. Coin in Bank of England reduced to £1,027,000.......	7	24	4	29
18	Sat	....	7	25	4	29
19	SUN	....	7	25	4	30
20	Mon	....	7	26	4	31
21	Tue	1620. The Pilgrims landed at Plymouth, Mass., (O. S., 11th.).	7	26	4	31
22	Wed	....	7	27	4	32
23	Thu	1847. Bank of Chester County robbed of $50,000 circulation.	7	27	4	32
24	Frid	1838. The New Orleans Banks resumed specie payments.....	7	28	4	33
25	Sat	1848. Peter C. Brooks died in Boston, aged 82.............	7	28	4	33
26	SUN	1831. Stephen Girard died at Philadelphia, aged 82........	7	28	4	34
27	Mon	....	7	29	4	35
28	Tue	....	7	29	4	35
29	Wed	1818. U. S. Bank Stock quoted at 109 to 110...............	7	29	4	36
30	Thu	1813. Buffalo burnt by the British......................	7	29	4	37
31	Frid	1829. Thomas Maynard hung—last criminal hung for forgery.	7	30	4	38

Bank Circulation.—On the whole it seems wiser to retain the established institutions of the country, instead of resorting to doubtful and hazardous experiments. What is wanted, I think, in our banking system, is this — first, to widen the basis of the metallic circulation, by abolishing the use of all small notes, so as to allow coin to take the place of them, as it inevitably would. And second, to annex to the non-payment of specie by the banks, so heavy a penalty, say an interest of 12 per cent., as in the Bank of the U. States, or 24 per cent., as in some of the Jersey banks, as would deprive the banks of all temptation to incur the risk of insolvency.—*N. Biddle.*

LAWSON'S EARLY HISTORY OF BANKING.

Contained in the Bankers' Magazine, 1851 – 52.

THE HISTORY OF BANKING; WITH A COMPREHENSIVE ACCOUNT OF THE ORIGIN, RISE, AND PROGRESS OF THE BANKS OF ENGLAND, IRELAND, AND SCOTLAND. By WILLIAM JOHN LAWSON. London: Richard Bentley.

WITHIN the last few years, and even since the establishment of our *Magazine*, the literature of banking has assumed a different character from that which it previously presented. The race of currency essayists has given place to the historians and statists. We are no longer inundated by pamphlets on the national debt and new systems of currency; and the old race of writers, who exhausted their own powers and their readers' patience in endeavoring to solve the problem, when the national debt would or could be extinguished, have now given place to a more interesting class of authors, who make facts and statistics the groundwork of their labors. We say nothing in disparagement of the old currency pamphleteers. Although they materially assisted in rendering "the currency question" a bugbear to those who had no hobby of their own on the subject, they did good service in the cause of truth by keeping the question continually before the public; and it would ill become those who are now benefiting by their labors, to disparage their exertions. But we confess we would rather have a few such works as Francis's "History of the Bank of England," and the volume before us, than many hundred volumes of the essays on banking and the currency which have previously been issued.

Mr. Lawson has given us a very interesting volume, as his contribution to the History of Banking. He has taken great pains to make his work accurate; and as it is the result of many years' labor and research, it possesses a higher value than could be claimed for a more ephemeral publication. He presents us with a good general view of the state of banking, and incidentally of commerce also, from the earliest periods to the present time; and he has interwoven his facts so pleasantly with anecdotal narrative, that the work will be found interesting by all classes of readers. — *London Bankers' Magazine.*

THE HISTORY OF BANKING; WITH A COMPREHENSIVE ACCOUNT OF THE ORIGIN, RISE, AND PROGRESS OF THE BANKS OF ENGLAND, IRELAND, AND SCOTLAND. By WILLIAM J. LAWSON.

From the London Spectator, September 28, 1850.

THIS volume has a wider range than some late books on banks and banking, or than its own title would imply. Taxes, and coin to pay them with, have existed in this country since the time of the Romans. As soon as there is sufficient order in society (lawless as it still may be) to warrant the journeys of a commercial traveller, the money-changer springs up in large towns; for without him a man might be in the position of Midas, and starve with gold and silver in his possession, or be fleeced more completely by the amateur than by the regular dealer, — as indeed is usually the case. How credit originates is not easily told; its beginning, like other indispensable acts, is lost in the lapse of ages. But credit proper — goods "upon tick" — perhaps arose nilly-willy; those took "who had the power," and satisfied their conscience with a promise to pay. Banking proper — the deposit of valuables for security, to be returned on demand — originated in trust, in the confidence the depositor felt in the honor of the person trusted. A money-order was perhaps antecedent to the money-changer, and if not anterior to writing itself, was anterior to it as a general accomplishment; a ring or other token answering the purpose of the modern check. The bill of exchange has been attributed by many, including David Hume, to the persecution of the Jews during the Middle Ages. That it had an Oriental origin is probable, but the thing itself must have been nearly contemporary with distant trade and deposited valuables. When the first money-order was transferred by the necessity or convenience of the holder, there was essentially a bill of exchange, though a modern lawyer or bill-broker might say no, on account of its want of form. As nations grew richer, trade increased, and law as a parallel cause was better enforced; credit, deposits, and that substitute for *ready* money, a bill of exchange, increased too; till the money-changer and goldsmith passed into the banker, and the law of bills and bankers' checks was established on the usages of trade. To effect this, took many ages in all countries; banking was practised in Italy some centuries before it was established in England; efforts were made by far-seeing men or by premature projectors to force public banks in England, more than half a century before the wants of the general public permitted success. The real growth of the system, when society was ripe for it, is read in the history of the house of Smith, Payne, and Smith.

Of all these topics — of ancient coins and coinage, primitive money-changing, bills of exchange, and banking in this country — Mr. Lawson gives what he calls a comprehensive account; but which strikes us as being rather a succinct summary, for it is not distinguished by much grasp or completeness. These things are followed by an elaborate history of the Bank of England, more legal and commercial than personal and anecdotal. English private banking in town and country succeeds to the story of the the Bank; next comes an account of the modern Joint-Stock Banks; and then the history of Scotch and Irish banking.

Of late years several works upon *banking* have appeared, whose main subject was similar to Mr. Lawson's; so that its leading outlines are not very new. Its greater range of topics and its peculiar treatment, however, give it some variety and even subordinate novelty. It is not so light as Francis's "History of the Bank of England," and some other books limited to stories, anecdotes, and strange incidents. If not so informing about the arcana of banking business, or so homogeneous in its treatment, as Gilbart's "History of Banking," its topics are somewhat loftier, involving ministerial and Parliamentary events.

Mr. Lawson himself is a practical banker, who has lived since he left the Blue-Coat School in the atmosphere of the "shop." His attention has been directed to the traditions of the craft, with which he varies his narrative.

CIRCULAR TO BANKING INSTITUTIONS.

The Publisher of the *Bankers' Magazine* gives notice that the following important and interesting works will be embodied in "*The Bankers' Magazine and Statistical Register*," for the year beginning July, 1851, and ending June, 1852: —

I. New Varieties of Gold and Silver Coins and Bullion, with important details relating to the Coinage, Rules of the Mint, &c. By Jacob R. Eckfeldt and W. E. Dubois, Assayers of the United States Mint.

II. The American Law of Banking. A Synopsis of the Decisions of the higher Courts of every State in the Union, upon the subjects of Banking, Bills of Exchange, Promissory Notes, Damages on Bills, Usury, Notaries Public, &c. The decisions of each State will be arranged by themselves, commencing with Maine; to be followed in order by New Hampshire, Vermont, Massachusetts, Connecticut, New York, &c.

III. History of Banking and Currency. By W. J. Lawson, Esq. A recent English Work.

IV. Historical Sketches of the Early Currency among the American Colonies.

V. Gilbart's Practical Treatise on Banking, — *concluded.* The Second American Edition of this work, *entire* (470 pages), may be had of booksellers throughout the United States.

The *Bankers' Magazine* is now published monthly, 84 pages, octavo, at Five Dollars per annum. By the new postage law of the United States, the postage on this work is essentially reduced.

The editor desires all communications and subscriptions to be *forwarded per mail*, and not by Express.

J. SMITH HOMANS, Editor Bankers' Magazine,
111 *Washington Street, Boston.*

POSTAGE, within 500 miles, 9 cts. per Quarter; between 500 and 1500 miles, 18 cts. per Quarter, payable in advance.

THE BANKERS' MAGAZINE, AND Statistical Register.

EDITED BY J. SMITH HOMANS.

"No expectation of forbearance or indulgence should be encouraged. Favor and benevolence are not the attributes of good banking. Strict justice and the rigid performance of contracts are its proper foundation."

"The Revenue of the State IS THE STATE: in effect, all depend upon it, whether for support or for reformation."

DECEMBER, 1851.—CONTENTS.

BOSTON:

PUBLISHED MONTHLY, BY J. SMITH HOMANS, 111 WASHINGTON STREET.

50 WALL STREET, NEW YORK.

Bank of British North America.

LONDON.

CAPITAL, £1,000,000 STERLING.

INCORPORATED BY ROYAL CHARTER.

Court of Directors.—Henry Barnewall, Esq.; Thomas H. Brooking, Esq.; Sir Robt. Campbell, Bart; Robt. Carter, Esq.; W. R. Chapman, Esq.; William Chapman, Esq.; James John Cummins, Esq.; James Dowie, Esq.; Oliver Farrer, Esq.; Alexander Gillespie, Esq.; Sir A. Pellet Green, R. N.; John Stewart, Esq. *Secretary*—George D. B. Attwood, Esq.

Inspector of Branches—Thomas Paton, Esq. *Agents in New York.*—Messrs. Richard Bell, Wm. McLachlan, and H. E. Ransom. *Branches of the B. B. N. A.*—Quebec, Montreal, Toronto, Kingston, Hamilton, Canada; Halifax, Nova Scotia; St. John, New Brunswick; St. Johns, Newfoundland. *Agencies in Canada*—Bytown, Brantford, Dundas.

Drafts on the B. B. N. A., London, and the Branches above; on the Branches of the Provincial Bank of Ireland; and National Bank of Scotland.

Bills of Exchange purchased and collected, and credits negotiated with England, Ireland, Scotland, and the British Provinces of North America, by Richard Bell, Wm. McLachlan, and H. E. Ransom, Agents, 43 Wall Street, New York.

August, 1851, 1y.

LAW AND AGENCY NOTICE.

CITY OF WASHINGTON.

WORTHINGTON G. SNETHEN

Continues to practice Law in the Supreme Court; to attend to cases before Congress; to prosecute Claims and settle accounts against the Departments and Boards of Commissioners; to procure Patents at home and abroad; to obtain Pensions and Bounty lands; to collect debts, dividends, legacies and inheritances in any part of the United States and in foreign countries; to make investments of funds in Loans and Stocks, and on Bond and Mortgage, and to negotiate the purchase and sale of Loans, Land and Patent rights in any State of the Union.

Particular attention paid to

CALIFORNIA LAND TITLE CASES,

coming up to the U. S. Supreme Court on appeal.

☞ Communications *prepaid*, addressed to

W. G. SNETHEN,

5 Carroll Place, Capitol Hill,

WASHINGTON, D. C.

will meet with prompt attention.

BANK NOTE ENGRAVING.

DANFORTH, BALD & CO.

Bank Note Engravers and Printers,

No. 1 WALL STREET, N. Y.—No. 95½ WALNUT ST. PHILADA.

NO. 78 STATE ST., BOSTON.

AND

FOURTH STREET, NEAR WALNUT, CINCINNATI.

Original designs for Vignettes and other embellishments furnished, when desired, without charge. *March*, 1851.

SMITH & BUTTLES'

IMPROVED

LETTER AND INVOICE FILE.

PATENT SECURED.

S & B LETTER FILE

MANUFACTURED AND FOR SALE BY

CROSBY & NICHOLS,

PUBLISHERS, BOOKSELLERS AND IMPORTERS,

AND

GENERAL AGENTS FOR ALL PERIODICALS,

111 Washington St., Boston.

This invaluable article not only combines every facility for ready reference, but a saving of much time and labor. By its use with Index, any Letters, Invoices, Bills, or other papers, of any date, may be found instanter, thus rendering it superior to all other methods. The prepared surface of the narrow leaves require only to be moistened, and the paper laid upon them.

All sizes made to order, and bound to match Account-Books, if desired.

☞ A liberal discount to the trade.

BLANK BOOKS, STAPLE and FANCY STATIONERY, SCHOOL, STANDARD, and useful MISCELLANEOUS WORKS, constantly on hand, and for sale at the lowest market cash prices.

JAMES L. LYELL,

Banking and Collecting Office,

DETROIT, MICHIGAN.

REFERS TO:

Messrs. Nevins, Townsend & Co., Cammann & Whitehouse, Strachan & Scott, *N. York.*

HOWARD & DAVIS,

34 WATER STREET, ... BOSTON, MASS.

MANUFACTURERS OF

GOLD STANDARD BALANCES,

FOR BANKS.

March, 1851.

PUTNAM'S
HOME CYCLOPÆDIA
IN SIX VOLUMES;

COMPRISING THE FOLLOWING:—EACH SOLD SEPARATELY.

HAND-BOOK OF LITERATURE AND FINE ARTS, by GEORGE RIPLEY, Esq., and BAYARD TAYLOR, Esq. 1 vol., 8vo, cloth, $2.00.

HAND-BOOK OF BIOGRAPHY, by PARKE GODWIN, Esq. 1 vol., 8vo, cloth, $2.00.

HAND-BOOK OF THE USEFUL ARTS, &c., by DR. ANTISELL. 1 vol., 8vo, $2.00.

HAND-BOOK OF THE SCIENCES, by Prof. ST. JOHN, of Western Reserve College. 1 vol., 8vo, cloth, $2.00.

HAND-BOOK OF GEOGRAPHY, or UNIVERSAL GAZETTEER.

HAND-BOOK OF HISTORY AND CHRONOLOGY, or THE WORLD'S PROGRESS: a Dictionary of Dates.

In all, 6 volumes, small 8vo, each containing from 600 to 800 pages, double columns, with Engravings.

The Hand-Book of Literature and the Fine Arts

Embraces all terms of Logic and Rhetoric, Criticism, Style, and Language; sketches of works which stand as types of their age or tongue; reviews of all systems of philosophy and theology, both of ancient and modern times; and a complete series of the history of literature among all nations, made up wholly from original sources. All the most important terms of common and international law, all technical words and phrases employed in theology and philosophy, and a number of scientific and historical phrases which have become familiarized in literature, have been included. The explanations are not confined to mere definitions; whenever it has been found necessary, illustrative woodcuts have been introduced, which will greatly assist the reader in his knowledge of architectural terms. In Art, the departments of Painting, Sculpture, and Architecture, have been treated as fully and carefully as the nature and limits of the work would permit. While a mere technical array of terms has been avoided, care has been taken to explain all the words, and phrases of art-criticism have been defined at some length, as of interest and value to the general reader, especially since criticism has been recognized as a distinct department of literature. All words relating to the art and practice of music have been likewise retained.

The Hand-Book of Biography

Is founded on Maunder's excellent work, the compiler having endeavored to preserve the compactness, while he has improved upon the fidelity and comprehensiveness of his original. He has re-written most of the articles, either to enlarge or condense them; and has added a vast number of names, especially of American men of eminence, and those who have died since former works were prepared. In all cases he has consulted the most reliable authorities, and given as much authentic information under each head as could be condensed into the allotted space.

The Hand-Book of the Useful Arts

Includes a description of the improvements and discoveries of the present advanced state of science, as well as a history of their gradual development. It will convey, as far as the limits of the volume will permit, the greatest possible amount of information concerning the subjects treated of, that could be combined in a work at once intended for popular use and private reference. Very many of the publications issued in this country have added little to the knowledge, previously existing in regard to its products, manufactures, or capabilities. Based, as all such works necessarily are, upon contemporaneous English productions, reference to the statistics and local peculiarities of this country is rarely found in their pages. It is hoped that in this Hand-Book of the Useful Arts, a step in advance has been made in chronicling the progress in Art to which the United States so rapidly and with such excellence have attained.

Dec. 1851.

Price, $1.00.

THE

MERCHANT'S AND BANKER'S

ALMANAC

FOR

1852.

CONTAINING,

I. Calendar and Chronology of Important Events.
II. The Banks of the United States in 1851. 1. Name and Location of each. 2. Names of President and Cashier of each. 3. Capital of each.
III. Synopsis of the Usury Laws, &c., of the States. 1. Legal Rates of Interest, and Penalties for the violation thereof. 2. Damages on Inland and Foreign Bills of Exchange. 3. Grace on Sight Bills. 4. Decisions of the State Courts.
IV. Coinage, Public Debt, Revenue, Expenditures, Post-offices, and Sales of Public Lands, of the United States, for each year from 1790 to 1850.
V. Public Debt, Revenue, and Expenditure of each State in the Union.
VI. Official Value of Foreign Coins at the Sub-Treasury and Custom-House of the U. S.
VII. Fluctuations of Stocks at New York and Baltimore each month in 1850.
VIII. Fluctuations of Stocks at Boston each month in 1849.
IX. Highest and Lowest Prices of English Funds each year from 1731 to 1848.
X. Highest and Lowest Prices of English Funds each month from 1847 to 1851.
XI. Table of Loans raised for Great Britain, and rates of Interest from 1793 to 1847.
XII. Rates of Exchange between New York and London each month from 1822 to 1850.
XIII. Forms of Bills of Exchange in Eight European Languages.
XIV. Tables of English and Scotch Money, during each reign, from 1066 to 1816.
XV. Tables of the Moneys of Account of various nations.
XVI. Tables of the Assay, Weight and Value of the Gold and Silver Coins of all nations.
XVII. The Bank of England. Directors from 1694 to 1847.
XVIII. Annual Dividends and Prices of Stock of the Bank of England from 1694 to 1847.
XIX. Public Debt, Revenue and Expenditure of the U. S. for the year ending June 30, 1850.
XX. Forms of Letters of Credit as used in New York and London for India Remittances.
XXI. The Banks of England, Ireland, and Scotland enumerated, with their Circulation and Coin.
XXII. List of the London Private Bankers and Members of the Clearing-House.
XXIII. Notes on a few Coins in general use.
XXIV. Sixty-five Engravings of recent American Coins.
XXV. Abstract of the Laws of the U. S. 1. Of the Mint. 2. Of Foreign Coins current in the U. S.
XXVI. Laws of the State of New York. 1. To organize a Bank Department. 2. The Bank Note Redemption Law. 3. New Insurance Law of New York.
XXVII. Miscellaneous Information.

To be Continued Annually.

PUBLISHED BY

PHILLIPS, SAMPSON & CO., 110 WASHINGTON STREET, BOSTON:
GEORGE P. PUTNAM, 155 BROADWAY, NEW YORK:
A. HART, PHILADELPHIA.

LAWRENCE SCIENTIFIC SCHOOL

OF HARVARD COLLEGE.

The ENGINEERING DEPARTMENT in this School has recently been established and organized under the superintendence of Professor HENRY L. EUSTIS, formerly Lieutenant in the Corps of Engineers in the United States Army, and Assistant Professor of Engineering at West Point. Provision is made for thorough instruction in all the branches of this Department.

Instruction in the other Departments is given as follows: —

CHEMISTRY, ... Professor HORSFORD.

The Laboratory is new, and one of the best constructed and most amply furnished in the world. Students have the use of it daily, under the direction of the Professor.

ZOÖLOGY AND GEOLOGY, ... Professor AGASSIZ.

ANATOMY AND PHYSIOLOGY, ... Professor WYMAN.

BOTANY AND VEGETABLE PHYSIOLOGY, ... Professor GRAY.

EXPERIMENTAL PHILOSOPHY, ... Professor LOVERING.

MATHEMATICS, including the DIFFERENTIAL CALCULUS and ANALYTICAL MECHANICS, } . Professor PEIRCE.

PRACTICAL ASTRONOMY, and the Use of Astronomical Instruments, } Mr. WM. C. BOND, Director of the Observatory, and Mr. GEORGE P. BOND, Assistant Observer.

Students have also access to the Library of the University, the Mineralogical, Geological, and Zoölogical Cabinets, and the Botanic Garden. Students in the Scientific School may attend without charge all the public lectures given to undergraduates.

LAW SCHOOL OF HARVARD COLLEGE.

This Institution affords a complete course of legal education for the Bar in any of the United States, excepting only matters of merely local law and practice; and also a systematic course of instruction in Commercial Law for those who propose to engage in Mercantile Pursuits.

The Law Library, which is constantly increasing, contains now about 14,000 volumes. It includes a very complete collection of American and English Law, and the principal works of the Civil and other foreign Law. It is open to students, and warmed and lighted for their use during both Terms and the Winter Vacation.

The First Term of each Academical Year begins in the last week of August, and the Second Term in the last week of February; each Term continues twenty weeks. Students are admitted at any period of a Term or Vacation. The fees are $50 a Term, and $25 for half a Term. For this sum, students have the use of the Law Library and text books, and of the College Library, and may attend all the courses of public lectures delivered to the undergraduates of the University.

The Instructors of the Law School are,

Hon. JOEL PARKER, LL.D., ... *Royall Professor.*

Hon. THEOPHILUS PARSONS, LL.D., .. *Dane Professor.*

Hon. LUTHER S. CUSHING, ... { *Lecturer on Real Law, the Civil Law, and Criminal Law.*

Instruction is given by Lectures, Recitations and Examinations, and Moot Courts.

For further information, application may be made to either of the Instructors.

JARED SPARKS, PRESIDENT.

CAMBRIDGE, APRIL, 1850.

IV. ESSAY ON PAPER MONEY AND BANKS.

CONTENTS.

CHAPTER I. — Utility of Paper Money.

CHAPTER II. — Security for Bank Issues.

CHAPTER III. — Classes of Banks.

CHAPTER IV. — Bank of England.

CHAPTER V. — JOINT STOCK BANKS OF GREAT BRITAIN.

CHAPTER VI. — THE SCOTCH BANKS.

CHAPTER VII. — THE IRISH BANKS.

CHAPTER VIII. — FOREIGN BANKS.

CHAPTER IX. — BANKING IN THE UNITED STATES.

www.ingramcontent.com/pod-product-compliance
Lightning Source LLC
LaVergne TN
LVHW021421110826
845150LV00007B/2031

* 9 7 8 1 4 2 5 5 0 9 3 5 4 *